D1486861

8

Show What You
COMMON CORE
the

Assessing Student Knowledge of the Common Core State Standards
(CCSS)

Reading

Show What You Know
Publishing

X

Published by:

Show What You Know® Publishing
A Division of Englefield & Associates, Inc.
P.O. Box 341348
Columbus, OH 43234-1348
Phone: 614-764-1211
www.showwhatyouknowpublishing.com

Standards are from the Common Core State Standards Initiative Web site at www.corestandards.org dated 2011.

Printed in the United States of America
13   12   11   20 19 18 17 16 15 14 13 12 11 10 9 8 7 6 5 4 3 2 1

ISBN: 1-59230-465-6

Acknowledgements

Show What You Know® Publishing acknowledges the following for their efforts in making this assessment material available for students, parents, and teachers:

Cindi Englefield, President/Publisher
Eloise Boehm-Sasala, Vice President/Managing Editor
Jennifer Harney, Editor/Illustrator

About the Contributors

The content of this book was written BY teachers FOR teachers and students and was designed specifically for the Common Core State Standards for Grade 8 Reading. Contributions to the Reading section of this book were also made by the educational publishing staff at Show What You Know® Publishing. Dr. Jolie S. Brams, a clinical child and family psychologist, is the contributing author of the Test Anxiety and Test-Taking Strategies chapters of this book. Without the contributions of these people, this book would not be possible.

Table of Contents

Introduction

Under the leadership of the National Governors Association (NGA) and the Council of Chief State School Officers (CCSSO), forty-eight states, two territories, and the District of Columbia joined the Common Core State Standards Initiative (CCSSI) in 2009.

The CCSSI has produced Common Core State Standards to provide uniformity and high standards for student achievement in grades K–12 across the nation. These core standards provide a consistent, clear understanding of what students are expected to learn, so teachers and parents have a roadmap for what they need to do to help them. Further, these standards provide appropriate benchmarks for all students, regardless of where they live, and allow states to more effectively help all students to succeed.

To develop these standards, CCSSO and the NGA worked with representatives from participating states, a wide range of educators, content experts, researchers, national organizations, and community groups. The adopted core standards reflect the invaluable feedback from the general public, teachers, parents, business leaders, states, and content area experts.

As reflected in our *Show What You Know® on the Common Core* Student Workbooks and Parent/Teacher Editions for grades 3–8, Reading and Mathematics are the first subjects chosen for the Common Core State Standards because these two subjects are skills upon which students build skill sets in other subject areas. They are also the subjects most frequently assessed for accountability purposes.

The *Show What You Know® on the Common Core* series for grades 3–8 is designed to review the new core standards and identify areas of students' strengths and needed improvement through diagnostic tests aligned to the core standards. In addition, the series provides chapters on test anxiety, test-taking strategies, and glossaries of terms for Reading and Mathematics to help prepare students with the knowledge and skills they need to succeed in the future.

Common Core State Standards will help ensure that students are receiving a high-quality education consistently, from school to school and state to state. These standards are a first step—a key building block—in providing students with a high-quality education that will prepare them for success in college and careers.

About the Show What You Know® Program

Show What You Know® Publishing has been developing test-preparation products since 1993. These products teach test-taking skills that are specific to state assessments and provide students with practice on full-length tests that simulate the format of state assessments. We understand that many students are not good test takers because they get nervous and may experience test anxiety. To help students with this issue, we provide a chapter, written by a child psychologist, that explains what test anxiety is, what it feels like, and ways to reduce the anxiety before, during, and after testing. Research has proven that three elements must exist for test success: knowledge, test-taking skills, and confidence. The Show What You Know® test-preparation program helps to ensure test success.

How to Use This Program

There are numerous ways to use the Student Workbook and Parent/Teacher Edition to help prepare your students for the Mathematics assessment. But before your students begin the assessments, take time to review the Test Anxiety and Test-Taking Strategies chapters in the Student Workbook to help them learn how to be better test takers. These important concepts can really improve students' test scores—it works!

Tips to Reduce Test Anxiety

You can read the entire chapter on test anxiety in the Student Workbook, or you can break it up into different sections, allowing yourself plenty of time to discuss and practice the methods suggested to reduce test stress. Identify what test anxiety is and help students learn the symptoms. Explain to them that test anxiety is normal, and that there are ways it can be overcome. Tell them how being a little nervous will motivate them to do their best, but being very nervous could make them forget information they need to know for the test.

The rest of the Test Anxiety chapter offers activities to show ways to overcome test stress, such as thinking positively instead of negatively, emphasizing the importance of good physical health, and studying and practicing for the test. These are skills that will help your students succeed on state assessments, as well as other tests your students will face throughout their lives.

Test-Taking Strategies That Work!

The Test-Taking Strategies chapter can be used in a class discussion. The chapter gives specific test-taking strategies for state assessments. After reviewing the chapter, ask students if they have found ways to help them prepare for tests. Maybe they like to read stories with their parents or they make sure to get extra sleep the week of a test. All of these strategies can be used to help them do well on state assessments and other tests.

The Purpose of the Assessments

After you have walked your students through the Test Anxiety and Test-Taking Strategies chapters, students can take two 40-question assessments for Reading.

These tests were designed to simulate state assessments so that students can become familiar with the actual look of the test. The more familiar students are with the look of the test, the more confidence they will have when they take the actual assessment.

Correlation Charts Track Students' Strengths and Weaknesses

In this Parent/Teacher Edition, there are Correlation Charts for each Assessment. The standards as well as test item answers are listed for each question. To use the chart, write the students' names in the left-hand column. When students miss a question, place an "X" in the corresponding box. A column with a large number of "Xs" shows that your class needs more practice with that particular standard. You can quickly identify the needs of individual students.

Answer Key with Sample Responses

Answers to the Reading assessments are provided in the Parent/Teacher Edition. The correct answer is given, and for short-answer questions, a sample response is offered.

Skills Chart

A skills chart for each assessment is provided in the Parent/Teacher Edition. The chart serves as a mini directory identifying the Common Core State Standard used for each assessment question, the correct answer choice, and the keyword(s) which summarize(s) the standard.

Additional Teaching Tools

A glossary of reading terms is provided in the Student Workbook to help your students understand terms that they should be familiar with in the eighth grade.

Suggested Timeline for Program Use

Now that you have a better understanding of how to use the Show What You Know® Test-Preparation Program, here is a suggested timeline for you to use to incorporate the program into your teaching schedule:

Suggested Timeline for Using the Show What You Know® on the Common Core for Grade 8 Reading, Student Workbook	
Week 1	Test Anxiety chapter
Week 2	Test-Taking Strategies chapter
Week 3	Review Glossary of Terms for Reading
Week 4	Reading Assessment One
Week 5	Additional Review After Results of Reading Assessment One
Week 6	Reading Assessment Two

Thank you for implementing the Show What You Know® Test-Preparation Program in your classroom. Good luck to you and all of your students as they prepare for their state assessments!

Test Anxiety

Introduction

The contents of the Test Anxiety chapter from the *Show What You Know® on the Common Core for Grade 8 Reading, Student Workbook*, begin on the next page. This chapter will help students begin to understand why they may feel some anxiety before taking a test. This anxiety is normal and is experienced by many people, not only students. The chapter offers information on different types of test takers and ideas on how to reduce worrisome feelings about tests.

What Does It Feel Like to Have Test Anxiety?

Students who have test anxiety don't always feel the same way, but they always feel bad. Here are some ways that students feel when they are anxious about tests.

- **Students who have test anxiety rarely think good things about themselves.**

  They lack confidence in their abilities, and they are convinced they will do poorly on tests. Not only do they feel bad about themselves and their abilities, but they just can't keep negative thoughts out of their minds. They would probably make terrible detectives, because in spite of all the good things they could find out about themselves, they only think about what they can't do. And that's not the worst of it. Students with test anxiety also exaggerate. When they think of the smallest problem, it becomes a hundred times bigger, especially when they think about tests. They are very unforgiving of themselves. If they make a mistake, they always think the worst or exaggerate the situation. If they do poorly on a quiz, they never say, "Well, it's just a quiz, and I'll try better next time." Instead they think, "That test was terrible and I can only imagine how badly I'll do next week." For students with test anxiety, there is never a brighter day ahead. They don't think many good thoughts about themselves, and they certainly don't have a happy outlook on their lives.

- **Students who have test anxiety have poor "thinking habits."**

  Negative thinking is a habit just like any other habit. Some habits are good and some habits are bad, but negative thinking is probably the worst habit of all. A habit forms when you do something over and over again until it becomes so much a part of you that you don't think about it anymore. Students with test anxiety get into bad thinking habits. They develop negative ways of thinking about themselves and about schoolwork, especially about tests. They tend to make the worst out of situations and imagine all kinds of possibilities that probably will not happen. Their thoughts grow like a mushroom out of control. Besides having negative ideas about tests, they begin to have negative ideas about almost everything else in their lives. This is not a good way of thinking because the more negative they feel about themselves, the worse they do in school, and bad grades make them feel even worse about themselves. What a mess. Students who have constant negative thoughts about themselves and schoolwork probably have test anxiety.

Test Anxiety

What is Test Anxiety?

Test anxiety is just a fancy name for feeling nervous about tests. Everyone knows what it is like to be nervous. Feeling nervous is not a good experience.

Many students have anxiety about taking tests, so if you are a test worrier, don't let it worry you. Most likely, many of your fellow students and friends also have fearful feelings about tests but do not share these feelings with others. Eighth grade is a time when everyone wants to seem "grown up," and few eighth graders want to look weak or afraid in the eyes of their friends or their teachers. But not talking to others about anxiety only makes the situation worse. It makes you feel alone and also makes you wonder if there is something "wrong" with you. Be brave! Talk to your friends and teachers about test anxiety. You will feel better for sharing.

Are You One of These "Test-Anxious" Eighth Graders?

As you have seen, students with test anxiety have negative thoughts about themselves, often feel anxious to the point of being ill, freak out and want to escape, and rarely show what they know on tests. Do any of the following kids remind you of yourself?

Stay-Away Stephanie

Stephanie's thoughts tell her it is better to stay away from challenges, especially tests. Stephanie is a good girl, but she is always in trouble at school for avoiding tests. Sometimes, she really feels ill and begs her mom to allow her to stay home on test days. At other times, Stephanie does anything to avoid school, refusing to get up in the morning or to leave the house to catch the bus. Stephanie truly believes there is nothing worse than taking a test. She is so overwhelmed with anxiety that she forgets about the problems that will happen when she stays away from her responsibilities. Unfortunately, the more she stays away, the worse the situation becomes. Stay-Away Stephanie feels less nervous when she doesn't face a test, but she never learns to face her fears.

Worried Wendy

Wendy is the type of eighth grader who always expects the worst thing to happen. She has many negative thoughts. Even when situations have turned out to be OK, Wendy focuses on the few bad things that happened. She exaggerates negative events and forgets about everything good. Her mind races a mile a minute with all sorts of thoughts and ideas about tests. The more she thinks, the worse she feels, and her problems become unbelievably huge. Instead of just worrying about a couple of difficult questions on a test, she finds herself thinking about failing the whole test, being made fun of by her friends, being grounded by her parents, and never going to college. She completely forgets that her parents would never be so strict, that her friends like her for many more reasons than her test grades, and that she has all sorts of career choices ahead of her. No one is going to hold it against her if she performed poorly on a test. It is not going to ruin her life. However, Wendy believes all of that would happen. Her negative thoughts get in the way of thinking anything positive.

• **Students who have test anxiety may feel physically uncomfortable or even ill.**
It is important to know that your mind and body are connected. What goes on in your mind can change how your body feels, and how your body feels can influence what goes on in your thinking. When students have test anxiety, their thoughts might cause them to have physical symptoms which include a fast heartbeat, butterflies in the stomach, headaches, and all sorts of other physical problems. Some kids become so ill they end up going to the doctor because they believe they are truly sick. Some students miss a lot of school due to anxiety, but they aren't really ill. Instead, their thoughts are controlling their bodies in a negative way. Some anxious students do not realize that what they are feeling is anxiety. They miss many days of school, not because they are lazy or neglectful, but because they believe they truly are not feeling well. Unfortunately, the more school they miss, the more behind they are and the more nervous they feel. Students who suffer from test anxiety probably feel even worse on test days. Their uncomfortable physical feelings will make them either avoid the test completely or feel so bad during the test that they do poorly. Guess what happens then. They feel even worse about themselves, become more anxious, and the cycle goes on and on.

• **Students who have test anxiety "freak out" and want to escape.**
Many students feel so bad when they are anxious that they will do anything to avoid that feeling. For most students, this means running away from problems, especially tests. Some students try to get away from tests by missing school. This does not solve any problems; the more a student is away from school, the harder schoolwork is, and the worse he or she feels. Some students worry about being worried. It may sound silly, but they are worried that they are going to freak out, and guess what happens . . . they do. They are so terrified that they will have uncontrollable anxious feelings that they actually get anxious feelings when thinking about this problem. For many students, anxiety is such a bad feeling that they will do anything not to feel anxious, even if it means failing tests or school. Although they know this will cause them problems in the future, their anxiety is so overwhelming they would rather avoid anxiety now and fail later. Unfortunately, this is usually what happens.

• **Students who have test anxiety do not show what they know on tests.**
Students who have test anxiety do not make good decisions on tests. Instead of focusing their thoughts, planning out their answers, and using what they know, students find themselves "blanking out." They stare at the paper, and no answer is there. They become "stuck" and cannot move on. Some students come up with the wrong answers because their anxiety gets in the way of reading directions carefully and thinking about answers thoughtfully. Their minds are running in a hundred different ways and none of those ways seem to be getting them anywhere. They forget to use what they know, and they also forget to use study skills that can help students do their best. When students are so worried that they cannot make good decisions and use all of the talents they have, it is called test anxiety.

How Do I Handle Test Anxiety?

Test anxiety is a very powerful feeling that convinces students they are weak and helpless. Feelings of test anxiety can be so powerful it seems there is nothing you can do to stop them. Anxiety seems to take over your mind and body and leaves you feeling like you are going to lose the test anxiety battle for sure.

The good news is that there are many simple things you can do to win the battle over test anxiety. If you can learn these skills in the eighth grade, you are on the road to success in school and for all other challenges in your life.

- **Change the Way You Think.**
  Most of us don't "think about how we think." We just go along thinking our thoughts and never really consider whether they are helpful or not helpful or if they are right or wrong. We rarely realize how much the way we think has to do with how well we get along in life. Our thoughts can influence how we feel about ourselves, how we get along with other people, how well we do in school, and how we perform on tests.

- **The Soda Pop Test.**
  Most eighth graders have heard a parent or teacher tell them, "There is more than one side to any story." One student reported that his grandfather used to say, "There's more than one way to paint a fence." Have you ever considered how you think about different situations? Most situations can be looked at in many ways, both good and bad.

Take a can of soda pop and put it on your desk or dresser at home. Get out a piece of paper and a pen or a pencil. Now, draw a line down the middle of the paper. On one side, put a heading: "All the bad things about this can of soda pop." On the other side put another heading: "All the good things about this can of soda pop." If you think about that can of soda pop, you might come up with the following chart.

All the bad things about this can of soda pop	All the good things about this can of soda pop
Not an attractive color	Easy-to-read lettering
It's getting warm	Nice to have something to drink
Not much in the can	Inexpensive
Has a lot of sugar	Recyclable aluminum cans

Critical Chris

Chris is the type of eighth grader who spends all of his time putting himself down. No matter what happens, he always feels he has been a failure. While some people hold grudges against others, Chris holds grudges against himself. No matter what little mistakes he makes, he can never forget them. Chris has had many good things happen to him in his life, and he has been successful many times. Unfortunately, Chris forgets all the good and only remembers the bad. Because he doesn't appreciate himself, Chris has test anxiety.

Victim Vince

Most eighth graders find it is important to take responsibility for their actions. It helps them understand that adulthood is just around the corner, and that they are smarter and more able than they ever thought they were. However, Vince is not like this. He can't take responsibility for himself at all. He thinks everything is someone else's fault and constantly complains about friends, parents, schoolwork, and especially tests. He tells himself, "They make those tests too hard." He sees the teachers as unfair, and he thinks life is generally against him. Vince does not feel there is anything he can do to help his situation, and there is little he thinks he can do to help himself with tests. Because he does not try to learn test-taking skills or to understand why he is afraid, he continues to feel hopeless and angry. Not surprisingly, he does poorly on tests, which only makes his thoughts about the world around him worse.

Perfect Pat

Everyone knows that there is more homework and responsibility in eighth grade than in previous grades. Everyone in the eighth grade needs to try his or her best, but no one should try as much as Pat does. All Pat does is worry. No matter what she does, it's never good enough. She will write book reports over and over and study for tests until she is exhausted. Trying hard is fine, but no matter what Pat does, she feels she has never done enough. Because she never accomplishes what she sets out to do (that would be impossible), she worries all the time. Her anxiety level gets higher and higher. The more anxious she becomes, the worse she does on tests. This just makes her study and worry more. What a terrible situation!

Look how easy it is to write down good things or bad things about a silly can of soda pop. That can of soda pop is not really good or bad, it's just a can of soda pop, but we can either look at it in a positive way or we can think about everything negative that comes to our minds. Doesn't the same thing hold true for tests? Tests are not good or bad in themselves. Tests are just a way to challenge us and see what we know. Challenges can be stressful, but they can also be rewarding. Studying for tests can be boring and can take up a lot of free time, but we can also learn a lot and feel great about ourselves when we study. The way you think about tests will help determine how you do in a test-taking situation. Most importantly, how you feel about tests is related to your level of anxiety about test taking. Students who have negative thoughts and feelings about tests become anxious. Students who think positively are less anxious. To reduce test anxiety, try thinking about tests and testing situations using a positive frame of mind.

- **All or Nothing Thinking.**

Nothing is ever as simple as it seems. Sometimes we convince ourselves something is going to be "awful" or "wonderful." Rarely does it turn out that way.

Trouble comes along when students think tests are going to be an "awful" experience. If you dread something happening, it is only going to make things worse. Also, you may be wrong. Nothing is as terrible as it seems. All the negative thoughts you have about the upcoming test cannot possibly be true. Thinking something is "awful" or "terrible" and nothing else only leads to trouble and failure. The more negative you feel about something, the worse things turn out.

Very few things are "all good" or "all bad." This is especially true for tests. Recognizing the "bad" parts of tests can help you be successful. For example, the fact that you need to study for tests, to pay attention while you are taking tests, and to understand there are probably many more fun things to do in school than take tests are all "true" thoughts. "Good" thoughts are just as true, including the good feelings one gets from studying and the chance that you might do well. Having "all or nothing" thinking is going to get you nowhere. Successful and happy students know some experiences are better than others, but they try to look at a situation from all sides.

- **Mind Reading.**

Some students believe they can read the minds of their parents and teachers. They assume if they do poorly on a test, everyone will think they are "dumb" or "lazy." The more their minds create all the terrible things that people may say about them, the more anxious they get. This just increases anxiety and definitely does not help students do well on tests.

- **Catastrophizing.**

When people catastrophize, they make everything a catastrophe. A catastrophe is a disaster. It is when something terrible happens. When a student catastrophizes, his or her mind goes on and on creating terrible scenes of disasters. If someone put all these ideas into a movie script, the writer might be rich.

Your state proficiency test is an important part of an eighth-grader's school year. It is a test that helps the student, the teacher, and the school. However, an eighth-grade student is much more than just his or her score on the test. Each student is an individual who has his or her own great personality, talents, and other successes in school. If what people catastrophized about was really true, the whole world would be a terrible mess. Imagine if your mother cooked a dinner that didn't turn out quite right. This might mean everyone has to go out for fast food, but you wouldn't love your mother any less. It would be catastrophizing if your mother said, "Now that I burned the dinner, none of my kids will love me. They will probably just want to move out as quickly as they can, and my life will be ruined." Catastrophizing about a test is just as bad. Thinking that this test is going to be the worst experience of your life and that your future will be ruined will not help you feel comfortable when preparing for and taking the test.

- **Making "Should" Statements.**

Students make themselves anxious when they think they "should" do everything. They feel they "should" be as smart as everyone else, "should" study more, and "should" not feel anxious about tests. All these thoughts are pretty ridiculous. You can't always be as smart as the next person, and you do not have to study until you drop to do well on tests. Instead of kicking yourself for not being perfect, it is better to think about all the good things you have done in your life. This will help you do better on tests and be happier in your life by reducing your anxiety.

How Do I Replace Worried Thoughts with Positive Ones?

As we have learned, there are all kinds of thoughts that make us anxious, such as feeling we "should" do everything, thinking we can read peoples' minds, catastrophizing, and thinking only bad thoughts about a situation. Learning how to stop these types of thoughts is very important. Understanding your thoughts and doing something about them help control test anxiety.

People who are worried or anxious can become happier when thinking positive thoughts. Even when situations are scary, such as a visit to the dentist, "positive imagery" is helpful. "Positive imagery" means thinking good thoughts to keep from thinking anxious thoughts. Positive and negative thoughts do not go together. If you are thinking something positive, it is almost impossible to think of something negative. Keep this in mind when test anxiety starts to become a bother.

Try these ideas the next time you find yourself becoming anxious.

- **Thoughts of Success.**
Thinking "I can do it" thoughts can chase away thoughts of failure. Imagine times you were successful, such as when you performed well in a dance recital or figured out a complicated brain teaser. These are good things to think about. Telling yourself you have been successful in the past and can be successful in the future will chase away thoughts of anxiety.

- **Relaxing Thoughts.**
Some people find that thinking calming or relaxing thoughts is helpful. Picturing a time in which you felt comfortable and happy can lessen your anxious feelings. Imagine yourself playing a baseball game, running through a park, or eating an ice cream cone; these are all positive thoughts that may get in the way of anxious ones. Some students find that listening to music on the morning of a test is helpful.
It probably doesn't matter what music you listen to, as long as it makes you feel good about yourself, confident, and relaxed.

Just as you can calm your mind, it is also important for you to relax your body. Practice relaxing your body. When students have test anxiety, their muscles become stiff. In fact, the whole body becomes tense. Taking deep breaths before a test and letting them out slowly as well as relaxing muscles in your body are all very helpful ways to feel less anxious. Your school counselors will probably have more ideas about relaxation. You may find that relaxation doesn't just help you on tests, but is helpful for other challenging situations and for feeling healthy overall.

- **Don't Let Yourself Feel Alone.**
Everyone feels more anxious when they feel alone and separate from others. Talking to your friends, parents, and teachers about your feelings helps. Feeling anxious about tests does not mean there is something wrong with you. You will be surprised to find that many of your friends and fellow students also feel anxious about tests. You may be even more surprised to learn your parents and teachers have also had test anxiety. They know what you are going through and are there to support you.

- **Take Care of Yourself.**
Everyone is busy. Many eighth graders are involved in all sorts of activities, including sports, music, and helping around the house. Often, you are so busy you forget to eat breakfast or you don't get enough sleep. Eating and sleeping right are important, especially before a test like your state proficiency test. If you are not a big breakfast eater, try to find something that you like to eat and get in the habit of eating breakfast. When you do not eat right, you may feel shaky and have a hard time concentrating, and your anxiety can increase. Being tired does not help either. Try to get in the habit of going to bed at a good time every night (especially the night before a test) so you can feel fresh, rested, and confident.

- **Practice Your Test-Taking Success.**
People who have accomplished incredibly difficult goals have used their imaginations to help them achieve success. They thought about what they would do step by step to be successful.

You can do the same. Think about yourself on the morning of the test. Imagine telling yourself positive thoughts and eating a good breakfast. Think about arriving at school and feeling confident that you will do fine on the test. Imagine closing your eyes before the test, breathing deeply, relaxing, and remembering all the study skills you have learned. The more you program your mind to think in a successful and positive way, the better off you will be.

- **Learn to Use Study Skills.**
The next chapter in this book will help you learn test-taking strategies. The more you know about taking tests successfully, the calmer you will feel. Knowledge is power. Practice test-taking strategies to reduce your test anxiety.

- **Congratulate Yourself During the Test.**
Instead of thinking, "I've only done five problems and I've got eight pages to go," or "I knew three answers were right but one mixed me up," "reward yourself for what you have done. Tell yourself, "I got some answers right so far, so I bet I can do more." After all, if you don't compliment yourself, who will?

Conclusion
You are not alone if you feel stressed about tests. It is probably good to feel a little anxious, because it motivates you to do well. However, if you feel very anxious about tests, then reading, re-reading, and practicing the suggestions in this chapter will help you "tackle your test anxiety."

Test-Taking Strategies

Introduction

The contents of the Test-Taking Strategies chapter, from the *Show What You Know® on the Common Core for Grade 8 Reading, Student Workbook*, begin on the next page. This chapter will introduce students to test-taking strategies. These strategies are hints students can use for any test, but they are especially helpful for state assessments. This chapter will give students the tools they need to become successful test takers.

Tools You Can Use on Tests Throughout Your Life!

Be An "Active Learner."

You can't learn anything by being a "sponge." Just because you are sitting in a pool of learning (your classroom) does not mean you are going to learn anything just by being there. Instead, students learn when they actively think and participate during the school day. Students who are active learners pay attention to what is being said. They also constantly ask themselves and their teachers questions about the subject. When able, they participate by making comments and joining discussions. Active learners enjoy school, learn more, feel good about themselves, and usually do better on tests. Remember the auto-repair mechanic? That person had a lot of knowledge about fixing cars. All the tools and strategies in the world will not help you unless you have benefited from what your teachers have tried to share.

Being an active learner takes time and practice. If you are the type of student who is easily bored or frustrated, it is going to take some practice to use your classroom time differently. Ask yourself the following questions.

- Am I looking at the teacher?
- Do I pay attention to what is being said?
- Do I have any questions or ideas about what the teacher is saying?
- Do I listen to what my fellow students are saying and think about their ideas?
- Do I work with others to try to solve difficult problems?
- Do I look at the clock and wonder what time school will be over, or do I appreciate what is happening during the school day and how much I can learn?
- Do I try to think about how my schoolwork might be helpful to me now or in the future?

Although you do need special tools and strategies to do well on tests, the more you learn, the better chance you have of doing well on tests. Think about Kristen.

> There was a young girl named Kristen,
> Who was bored and wouldn't listen.
> She didn't train
> To use her smart brain
> And never knew what she was missing!

Test-Taking Strategies

All Students Can Do Their Best on Tests!

Most students want to do their best on tests. Tests are one important way for teachers to know how well students are doing and for students to understand how much progress they are making in their studies. Tests, like your state proficiency test, help schools measure how well students are learning so teachers and principals can make their schools even better. Students can do the best job possible in "showing what they know" by learning how to be good test takers.

It's just not possible to do a good job without the right tools. Test-taking strategies are tools to help you perform well on tests. Everyone needs good tools and strategies when facing a problem. If you do not have these, even the smartest or most talented person will do poorly. Think about people who are "wizards" at fixing cars and trucks. Your family's car "dies" in the middle of the road. The situation looks pretty hopeless. How are you ever going to get to that basketball game tomorrow if your parent's car is a mechanical mess? Suddenly, "magic" happens. The mechanic at the repair shop calls your parents and tells them the car is ready, just a day after it broke down. How did this happen? It happened because the auto-repair mechanic had a great deal of knowledge about cars. Most importantly, he had the right tools and strategies to fix the car. He knew how to look at the problem, and when he figured out what to do, he had some special gadgets to get the job done. You also can find special ways that will help you be a successful test taker.

When you think about a test or any other academic challenge, try to focus on what you can learn step by step and day by day. You will be surprised how all of this learning adds up to make you one of the smartest eighth graders ever. Think about Ray.

There was a smart boy named Ray,
Who learned something new every day.
He was pretty impressed
With what his mind could possess.
His excellent scores were his pay!

Get to Know the Test.
Most eighth graders are probably pretty used to riding in their parents' cars. They know how to make the air conditioning cooler or warmer, how to change the radio stations, and how to adjust the volume on the radio. Think about being a passenger in a totally unfamiliar car. You might think, "What are all those buttons? How do I even turn on the air conditioner? How do I make the window go up and down?" Now, think about taking your state proficiency test. Your state proficiency test is a test, but it may be different than some tests you have taken in the past. The more familiar you are with the types of questions on the test and how to record your answers, the better you will do. Working through the reading chapter in this book will help you get to know the test. Becoming familiar with the test is a great test-taking tool. Think about Sue.

There was a kid named Sue,
Who thought her test looked new.
"I never saw this before!
How'd I get a bad score?"
If she practiced, she might have a clue!

Don't Depend on Luck.
Preparing for your state proficiency test might feel stressful or boring at times, but it is an important part of learning how to show what you know and doing your best. Even the smartest student needs to spend time taking practice tests and listening to the advice of teachers about how to do well. Luck alone is not going to help you do well on tests. People who depend on luck do not take responsibility for themselves. Some people who believe in luck do not want to take the time and effort to do well. It is easier for them to say, "It's not my fault I did poorly. It's just not my lucky day." Some people just do not feel very good about their abilities. They get in the habit of saying, "Whatever happens will happen." They believe they can never do well no matter how much they practice or prepare. Students who feel they have no control over what happens to them usually have poor grades and do not feel very good about themselves.

Your performance on tests is not going to be controlled by luck. Instead, you can have a lot of control over how well you do in many areas of your life, including test taking. Don't be like Chuck.

There was a cool boy named Chuck,
Who thought taking tests was just luck.
He never prepared.
He said, "I'm not scared."
When his test scores appear, he should duck!

Do Your Best Every Day.
Many students find eighth grade much different than other grades. Suddenly, the work seems really hard. Not only that, but your teachers are no longer treating you like a baby. That's good in some ways, because it gives you more freedom and responsibility, but there sure is a lot to learn. You might feel the same way about tests; you may feel you'll never be prepared. Many times when we are faced with new challenges, it is easy just to give up.

Students are surprised when they find that if they just set small goals for themselves, they can learn an amazing amount. If you learn just one new fact every day of the year, at the end of the year, you will know 365 new facts. You could use those to impress your friends and family. Now think about what would happen if you learned three new facts every day. At the end of the year, you would have learned 1,095 new facts. Soon you will be on your way to having a mind like an encyclopedia.

Learning how to fill in answer bubbles takes practice, practice, and more practice. It may not be how you are used to answering multiple-choice questions, but it is the only way to give a right answer on your state proficiency test. Think about Kay!

> A stubborn girl named Kay,
> Liked to answer questions her own way.
> So her marked answer bubbles,
> Gave her all sorts of troubles.
> Her test scores ruined her day!

Speeding Through the Test Doesn't Help.
Most students have more than enough time to read and answer all the questions on a test. There will always be some students who finish the test more quickly than others, but this does not mean the test was easier for them or their answers are correct. Whether you finish at a faster rate or at a slower rate than other students in your class is not important. As long as you take your time, are well prepared, concentrate on the test, and use some of the skills in this book, you should be able to do just fine. You will not get a better score just because you finish the test before everyone else. Speeding through a test item or through a whole test does not help you do well. In fact, students do their best when they work at a medium rate of speed, not too slow and not too fast. Students who work too slowly tend to get worried about their answers and sometimes change correct answers into incorrect ones. Students who work too fast often make careless mistakes, and many of them do not read directions or questions carefully. Think about Liz.

> There was a eighth grader named Liz.
> Who sped through her test like a whiz.
> She thought she should race
> At a very fast pace,
> But it caused her to mess up her quiz.

Read Directions and Questions Carefully!
One of the worst mistakes a student can make on a test is to ignore directions or to read questions carelessly. By the time some students are in the eighth grade, they think they have heard every direction or question ever invented, and it is easy for them to "tune out" directions. Telling yourself, "These directions are just like other directions," or "I'm not really going to take time to read this question because I know what the question will be," are not good test-taking strategies. It is impossible to do well on any test without knowing what is being asked.

Reading directions and questions slowly, repeating them to yourself, and asking yourself if what you are reading makes sense are powerful test-taking strategies. Think about Fred.

> There was a nice boy named Fred,
> Who ignored almost all that he read.
> The directions were easy,
> But he said, "I don't need these!"
> He should have read them instead.

Know How to Fill in Those Answer Bubbles!
Most eighth graders have taken tests that ask them to fill in answer bubbles. You might be a very bright eighth grader, but you will never "show what you know" unless you fill in the answer bubbles correctly. Don't forget: a computer will be "reading" your multiple-choice question answers. If you do not fill in the answer bubble darkly or if you use a check mark or dot instead of a dark mark, your smart thinking will not be counted. Look at the examples given below.

Correct

Incorrect

Practice Here

Answer Every Question.

There is no reason that you should not attempt to answer every question you encounter on a test. Even if you don't know the answer, there are ways for you to increase your chances of choosing the correct response. Use the helpful strategies described below to help you answer every question to the best of your ability.

• **If you don't know the answer, guess.**
Did you know that on your state proficiency test there is no penalty for guessing? That is really good news. That means you have a one out of four chance of getting a multiple-choice question right, even if you just close your eyes and guess. That means that for every four questions you guess, you should get about 25% (1 out of 4) of the questions right. Guessing alone is not going to make you a star on the test, but leaving multiple-choice items blank is not going to help you either.

Now comes the exciting part. If you can rule out one of the four answer choices, your chances of answering correctly are now one out of three. You can almost see your test score improving right before your eyes.

Although it is always better to be prepared for the test and to study in school, we all have to guess at one time or another. Some of us do not like to guess because we are afraid of choosing the wrong answer, but on a test, it is better to guess than leave an answer blank. Think about Jess.

There was a smart girl named Jess,
Who thought it was useless to guess.
If a question was tough,
She just gave up.
This only added to her stress.

• **Use a "code" to help you make good guesses.**
Some students use a "code" to rate each answer when they feel they might have to guess. Using your pencil in the test booklet, you can mark the following codes next to each multiple-choice response so you can make the best possible guess. The codes are as follows:

(+) Putting a "plus sign" by your answer means you are not sure if this answer is correct, but you think this answer is probably more correct than the others.

(?) Putting a "question mark" by your answer means you are unsure if this is the correct answer, but you don't want to rule it out completely.

(−) Putting a "minus sign" by your answer means you are pretty sure this is the wrong answer. You should then choose from the other answers to make an educated guess.

Remember, it is fine to write in your test booklet. Think about Dwight.

There was a smart kid named Dwight,
Who marked answers that looked to be right.
He'd put a plus sign
Or a dash or a line.
Now the whole world knows he is bright!

• **Use what you know to "power guess."**
Not everything you know was learned in a classroom. Part of what you know comes from just living your life. When you take a test, you should use everything you have learned in school, but you should also use your experiences outside the classroom to help you answer questions correctly. Using your "common sense," as well as other information you know, will help you do especially well on a test. Try to use what you know from the world around you to eliminate obviously wrong answers. If you can rule out just one answer that you are certain is not correct, you are going to greatly increase your chances of guessing another answer correctly. For example, if you are given a question in which you are asked the definition of a word, and one of the answers reminds you of something you saw on TV, you might be able to count that answer out using your own experiences. Although the reading might be difficult for you, your common sense has eliminated one likely wrong answer. Think about Drew.

There was a boy named Drew,
Who forgot to use what he knew.
He had lots of knowledge.
He could have been in college!
But his right answers were few.

- **Do Not Get Stuck on One Question.**

One of the worst things you can do on a test is to get stuck on one question. Your state proficiency test gives you many chances to show all that you have learned. Not knowing the answer to one or two questions is not going to hurt your test results very much.

When you become stuck on a question, your mind plays tricks on you. You begin to think that you are a total failure, and your worries become greater and greater. This worrying gets in the way of your doing well on the rest of the test. Remember, very few students know all the answers on a test. If you are not sure of the answer after spending some time on it, mark it in your test booklet and come back to it later. When you come back to that question later, you might find a new way of thinking. Sometimes, another question or answer later in the test will remind you of a possible answer to the question that had seemed difficult. If not, you can use your guessing strategies to solve the questions you are unsure of after you have answered all the questions you know. Also, when you move on from a troubling question and find you are able to answer other questions correctly, you will feel much better about yourself and you will feel calmer. This will help you have a better chance of succeeding on a question that made you feel "stuck." Think about Von.

There was a sweet girl named Von,
Who got stuck and just couldn't go on.
She'd sit there and stare,
But the answer wasn't there.
Before she knew it, all the time was gone.

- **Always, and This Means Always, Recheck Your Work.**

Everyone makes mistakes. People make the most mistakes when they feel a little worried or rushed. Checking your work is a very important part of doing your best. This is particularly true in the reading section, where careless mistakes can lead to a wrong answer. Going back and rechecking your answers is very important. You can read a paragraph over again if there is something you do not understand or something that you forgot. If an answer does not seem to make sense, go back and reread the question. Think about Jen.

There was a quick girl named Jen,
Who read stuff once and never again.
It would have been nice
If she'd reread it twice.
Her test scores would be better then!

- **Pay Attention to Yourself and Not Others.**

It is easy to look around the room and wonder how friends are doing. However, it is important to think about how you are using tools and strategies. Don't become distracted by friends. You are going to waste a lot of time if you try to figure out what your friends are doing. Instead, use that time to "show what you know."

If it becomes hard for you to pay attention, give yourself a little break. If you feel you are getting a little tense or worried, or if a question seems tough, close your eyes for a second or two. Think positive thoughts. Try to put negative thoughts out of your mind. You might want to stretch your arms or feet or move around a little to help you focus. Anything you may do to help pay better attention to the test is a great test-taking strategy. Think about Kirk.

There was a boy named Kirk,
Who thought of everything but his work.
He stared into the air
And squirmed in his chair.
When his test scores come, he won't look!

Specific Strategies for Online Tests

Kids usually have two different kinds of thoughts about taking a test on a computer. Some say, "Well, I use my computer all the time … I'm not going to even pay attention to the test … computers are easy!" Some kids think in the opposite way. They say, "A computer test? That has to be even scarier than a regular test … there is no way I am going to do well!" The truth is that both of them are wrong. You have to use some special strategies to do your best on computer tests, and when you do, you will do your best!

1. **Read the Directions.** Here is a silly question: Would you want to eat a cake your friend made if she didn't read the directions on the box? Probably not! But even if you aren't a famous cook, you could make a pretty good cake if you read and follow directions. If you read the directions for EACH QUESTION you will have a much better chance of showing what you know. Because even if you know a lot, you have to answer what the question asks. Don't leave out this important step to test success!

2. **Don't Go With the First Answer.** Take a little time and read the WHOLE question and ALL the answer choices. The first answer that looks right is not always the best. Think about going out to dinner with your grandmother. You look at the menu and see "Big Ole Burger"! That sounds good. But if you looked at ALL the menu choices, you might have found your favorite tacos! The burger was good, but if you took more time, you would have found a better choice.

3. **Ask Yourself … How Much Time Do I Have?** You will have a certain amount of time to complete each section of the test. Always check to see how much time you will have. Practice also helps. Did you know that football players practice and practice to see how long it takes to line up and start a play? After a while they are more relaxed and don't worry about time running out. You need to take some practice tests to feel comfortable with timed tests.

4. **Is There a Good Way to Guess?** Most of the time it is a good idea to guess, especially if you can make an "educated" guess! That means you know some things about the question, but not everything. Remember to use your common sense, as well as other information you know, to help you make an "educated guess."

General Test-Taking Strategies for Reading

There are multiple-choice and short-answer questions on the Reading Assessment in this workbook. Here are some good strategies to use on the Reading Assessment.

*   **Read the Question Carefully.**

    It may help to look over the questions before you read through the passage. As you read the passage, look for information that may help you answer the questions.

*   **Look for Keywords.**

    Remember, you can write in your test booklet. As you read through the different passages, circle or underline important words you come across. Make notes in the margin with ideas that seem to answer the question.

*   **Review What You Read to Find More Details.**

    If you don't think you can answer the question, reread the passage and look for more details.

*   **Ask Yourself, "Did I Answer the Question?"**

    Read the answer choice you think is correct to make sure you have answered the question correctly.

*   **Circle the Numbers of the Questions You Cannot Answer.**

    If you are not sure of the correct answer, circle the question number and return to it later in the test.

*   **Do Not Immediately Pick Your First Answer.**

    Your first choice could be the correct choice, but it could also be a wrong answer that a test maker used to distract you. Recheck your answers.

---

5. When Should You Guess? Unless the directions say that you will lose points for guessing, go for it! Educated guesses are the best, but even if you are really unsure of the answer, calm down and take a guess. If you have four possible answers, and make a guess, you have a one out of four chance of guessing correctly. That is like having three old pennies and one new penny in a bowl. If you just reach in, you will get the new penny one out of every four times you try. That's why you should answer every question!

6. Don't Mess With That Test Window! When people get a little nervous, they tend to make silly mistakes. One kid was rushing to make some toast before running off to school, and he unplugged the toaster instead of making the toast! Figure out how the computer screen works, and DON'T close that test window!

7. Have a Good Attitude! The better you feel, the better you will do! Remind yourself of how much you have learned in school. Remember that while this test is important, your teachers will still like you a lot no matter how you do. Just do your best and feel good about yourself. Did you know that when runners have a good attitude, that they win more often? Well, the same goes for you and tests!

8. If You Have Time Left, Use It! You can use extra time to help you do your best! If your computer test allows, review your answers, especially if you guessed on a question or two. Take a deep breath and calm down. You might find that a better answer comes into your mind. Talk to yourself a little about some of your answers. You might ask yourself, "I chose the answer that said that it will take 6 hours for that ice cube to melt. That seems like a long time … maybe I better recheck this and see if that makes sense."

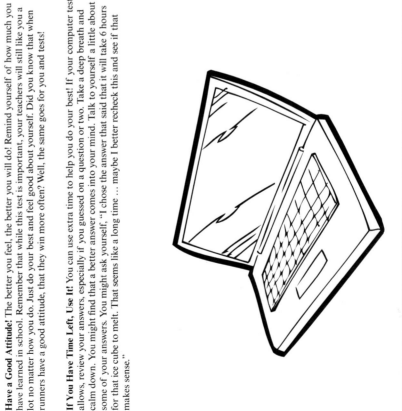

Eighth graders all over have good ideas about tests. Here are some of them!

- Ask yourself, "Did I answer the question that was asked?" Carefully read the question so you can give the right answer.

- Read each answer choice before filling in an answer bubble. Sometimes, you read the first choice, and it seems right. But, when you get to the third choice, you realize that's the correct answer. If you had stopped with the first choice, you would have answered the question incorrectly. It is important to read all four choices before answering the question.

- Remember, nobody is trying to trick you. Do not look for trick answers. There will always be a right answer. If the answer choices do not look right, mark the question and go back to it later.

- Don't look around the room. Don't worry about how fast your friends are working, and don't worry about how well they are doing. Only worry about yourself. If you do that, you will do better on the test.

Reading

Introduction

The Reading assessment reflects what students should know and should be able to do in the eighth grade. State assessments assess students' knowledge with multiple-choice and constructed-response items. The questions are not meant to confuse or trick them but are written so students have the best opportunity to show what they know about reading.

The Reading chapter in the *Show What You Know® on the Common Core for Grade 8 Reading, Parent/Teacher Edition,* contains the following:

- The Common Core State Standards for Grade 8 Reading.

- Two full-length Reading Assessments from the Student Workbook, in reduced-page format, with sample responses, correlation charts, a standards checklist, and a grading document.

Reading Standards for Literature (RL)

The following standards offer a focus for instruction each year and help ensure that students gain adequate exposure to a range of texts and tasks. Rigor is also infused through the requirement that students read increasingly complex texts through the grades. Students advancing through the grades are expected to meet each year's grade-specific standards and retain or further develop skills and understandings mastered in preceding grades.

Key Ideas and Details

1. Cite the textual evidence that most strongly supports an analysis of what the text says explicitly as well as inferences drawn from the text.

2. Determine a theme or central idea of a text and analyze its development over the course of the text, including its relationship to the characters, setting, and plot; provide an objective summary of the text.

3. Analyze how particular lines of dialogue or incidents in a story or drama propel the action, reveal aspects of a character, or provoke a decision.

Craft and Structure

4. Determine the meaning of words and phrases as they are used in a text, including figurative and connotative meanings; analyze the impact of specific word choices on meaning and tone, including analogies or allusions to other texts.

5. Compare and contrast the structure of two or more texts and analyze how the differing structure of each text contributes to its meaning and style.

6. Analyze how differences in the points of view of the characters and the audience or reader (e.g., created through the use of dramatic irony) create such effects as suspense or humor.

Integration of Knowledge and Ideas

7. Analyze the extent to which a filmed or live production of a story or drama stays faithful to or departs from the text or script, evaluating the choices made by the director or actors.

8. (Not applicable to literature)

9. Analyze how a modern work of fiction draws on themes, patterns of events, or character types from myths, traditional stories, or religious works such as the Bible, including describing how the material is rendered new.

Range of Reading and Level of Text Complexity

10. By the end of the year, read and comprehend literature, including stories, dramas, and poems, at the high end of grades 6–8 text complexity band independently and proficiently.

Reading Standards for Informational Text (RL)

Key Ideas and Details

1. Cite the textual evidence that most strongly supports an analysis of what the text says explicitly as well as inferences drawn from the text.

2. Determine a central idea of a text and analyze its development over the course of the text, including its relationship to supporting ideas; provide an objective summary of the text.

3. Analyze how a text makes connections among and distinctions between individuals, ideas, or events (e.g., through comparisons, analogies, or categories).

Craft and Structure

4. Determine the meaning of words and phrases as they are used in a text, including figurative, connotative, and technical meanings; analyze the impact of specific word choices on meaning and tone, including analogies or allusions to other texts.

5. Analyze in detail the structure of a specific paragraph in a text, including the role of particular sentences in developing and refining a key concept.

6. Determine an author's point of view or purpose in a text and analyze how the author acknowledges and responds to conflicting evidence or viewpoints.

Integration of Knowledge and Ideas

7. Evaluate the advantages and disadvantages of using different mediums (e.g., print or digital text, video, multimedia) to present a particular topic or idea.

8. Delineate and evaluate the argument and specific claims in a text, assessing whether the reasoning is sound and the evidence is relevant and sufficient; recognize when irrelevant evidence is introduced.

9. Analyze a case in which two or more texts provide conflicting information on the same topic and identify where the texts disagree on matters of fact or interpretation.

Range of Reading and Level of Text Complexity

10. By the end of the year, read and comprehend literary nonfiction at the high end of the grades 6–8 text complexity band independently and proficiently.

Glossary

alliteration: Repeating the same sound at the beginning of several words in a phrase or sentence. For example, "The bees buzzed in the back of the blue barn."

adjectives: Words that describe nouns.

adverbs: Words that describe verbs.

antonyms: Words that mean the opposite (e.g., *light* is an antonym of *dark*).

audience: The people who read a written piece or hear the piece being read.

author's purpose: The reason an author writes, such as to entertain, to inform, or to persuade.

author's tone: The attitude the writer takes toward an audience, a subject, or a character. Tone is shown through the writer's choice of words and details. Examples of tone are happy, sad, angry, gentle, etc.

base word (also called root word): The central part of a word that other word parts may be attached to.

biography: A true story about a person's life.

cause: The reason for an action, feeling, or response.

character: A person or an animal in a story, play, or other literary work.

compare: To use examples to show how things are alike.

contrast: To use examples to show how things are different.

details: Many small parts which help to tell a story.

descriptive text: To create a clear picture of a person, place, thing, or idea by using vivid words.

directions: An order or instructions on how to do something or how to act.

draw conclusion: To make a decision or form an opinion after considering the facts from the text.

effect: A result of a cause.

events: Things that happen.

fact: An actual happening or truth.

fiction: A passage that is made up rather than factually true. Examples of fiction are novels and short stories.

format: The way a published piece of writing looks, including the font, legibility, spacing, margins, and white space.

generalize: To come to a broad idea or rule about something after considering particular facts.

genres: Categories of literary and informational works (e.g., biography, mystery, historical fiction, poetry).

graphic organizer: Any illustration, chart, table, diagram, map, etc., used to help interpret information about the text.

heading: A word or group of words at the top or front of a piece of writing.

infer: To make a guess based on facts and observations.

inference: An important idea or conclusion drawn from reasoning rather than directly stated in the text.

inform: To give knowledge; to tell.

informational text (also called expository text): Text with the purpose of telling about details, facts, and information that is true (nonfiction). Informational text is found in textbooks, encyclopedias, biographies, and newspaper articles.

literary devices: Techniques used to convey an author's message or voice (e.g., figurative language, simile, metaphors, etc.).

literary text (also called narrative text): Text that describes actions or events, usually written as fiction. Examples are novels and short stories.

main idea: The main reason the passage was written; every passage has a main idea. Usually you can find the main idea in the topic sentence of the paragraph.

metaphor: A comparison between two unlike things without using the words "like" or "as." An example of a metaphor is, "My bedroom is a junkyard!"

Glossary

mood: The feeling or emotion the reader gets from a piece of writing.

nonfiction: A passage of writing that tells about real people, events, and places without changing any facts. Examples of nonfiction are an autobiography, a biography, an essay, a newspaper article, a magazine article, a personal diary, and a letter.

onomatopoeia: The use of words in which the sound of the word suggests the sound associated with it. For example, buzz, hiss, splat.

opinion: What one thinks about something or somebody; an opinion is not necessarily based on facts. Feelings and experiences usually help a person form an opinion.

passage: A passage or writing that may be fiction (literary/narrative) or nonfiction (informational/ expository).

persuade: To cause to do something by using reason or argument; to cause to believe something.

plan: A method of doing something that has been thought out ahead of time.

plot: A series of events that make up a story. Plot tells "what happens" in a story, novel, or narrative poem.

plot sequence: The order of events in a story.

poetry: A type of writing that uses images and patterns to express feelings.

point of view: The way a story is told; it could be in first person, omniscient, or in third person.

predict: The ability of the reader to know or expect that something is going to happen in a text before it does.

prefix: A group of letters added to the beginning of a word. For example, *untie, rebuild, preteen.*

preposition: A word that links another word or group of words to other parts of the sentence. Examples are in, on, of, at, by, between, outside, etc.

problem: An issue or question in a text that needs to be answered.

published work: The final writing draft shared with the audience.

reliable: Sources used for writing that are trustworthy.

resource: A source of help or support.

rhyme: When words have the same last sound. For example, hat/cat, most/toast, ball/call.

root word (also called base word): The central part of a word that other word parts may be attached to.

schema: The accumulated knowledge that a person can draw from life experiences to help understand concepts, roles, emotions, and events.

sentence: A group of words that express a complete thought. It has a subject and a verb.

sequential order: The arrangement or ordering of information, content, or ideas (e.g., a story told in chronological order describes what happened first, then second, then third, etc.).

setting: The time and place of a story or play. The setting helps to create the mood in a story, such as inside a spooky house or inside a shopping mall during the holidays.

simile: A comparison between two unlike things, using the words "like" or "as." "Her eyes are as big as saucers" is an example of a simile.

solution: An answer to a problem.

stanzas: Lines of poetry grouped together.

story: An account of something that happened.

story elements: The important parts of the story, including characters, setting, plot, problem, and solution.

style: A way of writing that is individual to the writer, such as the writer's choice of words, phrases, and images.

suffix: A group of letters added to the end of a word. For example, teach*er*, color*ful*, sugar*less*, etc.

summary: To retell what happens in a story in a short way by telling the main ideas, not details.

Glossary

supporting details: Statements that often follow the main idea. Supporting details give you more information about the main idea.

symbolism: Something that represents something else. For example, a dove is a symbol for peace.

synonyms: Words with the same, or almost the same, meaning (e.g., *sketch* is a synonym of *draw*).

theme: The major idea or topic that the author reveals in a literary work. A theme is usually not stated directly in the work. Instead, the reader has to think about all the details of the work and then make an inference (an educated guess) about what they all mean.

title: A name of a book, film, play, piece of music, or other work of art.

tone: A way of writing that shows a feeling.

topic sentence: A sentence that states the main idea of the paragraph.

valid: Correct, acceptable.

verb: A word that shows action or being.

voice: To express a choice or opinion.

Show What You Know® on the Common Core for Grade 8 Reading — Assessment One

Reading Assessment One

Responses *Throughout this section, pages from Reading Assessment One of the Student Workbook are included in reduced-page format. Correct multiple-choice answers and sample responses for each constructed-response item are indicated.*

Reading Assessment One

Directions for Taking the Reading Assessment

The Reading Assessment contains six reading selections and 40 questions. Some of the selections are fiction, while others are nonfiction. Read each selection and the questions that follow carefully. You may look back at any selection as many times as you would like. If you are unsure of a question, you can move to the next question, and go back to the question you skipped later.

Multiple-choice questions require you to pick the best answer out of four possible choices. Only one answer is correct. The short-answer questions will ask you to write your answer and explain your thinking using words. Remember to read the questions and the answer choices carefully. You will mark your answers on the answer document.

When you finish, check your answers.

Directions:

This Grade 8 Reading Assessment has multiple-choice and short-answer questions.

There are several important things to remember as you take this test:

- Read each multiple-choice question carefully. Think about what is being asked. Then fill in one answer bubble to mark your answer.

- If you do not know the answer to a multiple-choice question, skip it and go on. If you have time, go back to the questions you skipped and answer them.

- For short-answer questions, write your response clearly and neatly in the box provided.

- If you finish the Assessment early, go back and check over your work.

Read this selection. Then answer the questions that follow.

Them bones, them bones

1   Archaeologists and anthropologists are key players in our quest to understand the history of our world, from the evolution of man to the cultures of lost civilizations. The techniques developed in these two fields reach far into the past, but they also have critical applications in modern life.

2   Archaeology is the study of the lives and cultures of the past through the excavation of ancient grounds and the study of relics and artifacts. Anthropologists study the physical and cultural characteristics of humans, past and present. Cultural anthropologists specialize in the study of cultures, customs, and societies of people. Physical anthropologists concentrate on the physical characteristics of humans: bones, muscles, organs, and skin.

3   Archaeologists and anthropologists are frequently in the news. Human remains and artifacts are discovered by archaeologists at historic dig sites, or may be unearthed during excavation for construction. In these cases, archaeologists and anthropologists work to determine the era—the time period when the person or animal lived and died— of the remains, as well as the age, sex, race, and physical condition of the bodies. In cases where a complete skull is unearthed, physical anthropologists can frequently reconstruct the face of the deceased. This process involves using precise measurements based on known characteristics and reconstructing the facial features using clay built up on a cast of the skull. This process also can be completed more quickly using computer-generated pictures.

4   Artifacts are studied to examine lifestyle, jobs, wealth, and habits. This information is combined with known studies about cultures, in an effort to pinpoint the era of the excavated site. New discoveries help us to understand the cultural evolution of different regions and peoples.

5   Today, the methods developed by archaeologists and anthropologists are frequently used by the police. Physical anthropologists are frequently able to identify an unknown corpse or use age-progression processes to picture the face of a missing person who has aged. These skills have helped investigators find missing children and have contributed to solving many previously unsolved murders.

▲ Go On

---

1. From the author's point of view, archaeologists and anthropologists are important because—

   ✗ A. they are key players in our quest to understand the history of our world.

   B. they have helped the police to solve unsolved mysteries.

   C. anthropologists specialize in the study of culture, customs, and societies.

   D. they are frequently "in the news."

2. Which statement best supports the main idea that anthropologists have developed techniques beneficial to society?

   A. Anthropology is the study of lives and culture.

   B. Artifacts are used to study previous cultures.

   ✗ C. Anthropologists can reconstruct the face of a skeleton.

   D. Archaeological tools are now more advanced.

3. Read the sentence from the selection.

   "Archaeology is the study of the lives and cultures of the past through the excavation of ancient grounds and the study of *relics* and artifacts."

   The word *relics* means—

   ✗ A. remains.

   B. souvenirs.

   C. pieces.

   D. documents.

▲ Go On

Read this selection. Then answer the questions that follow.

School Schedule Shakeup

1   I am writing in response to the school board's recent decision to adjust Upper Valley's daily schedule for next year. The decision reduced the number of class periods each day from six to five. All study hall times have been eliminated. Our lunch break has been cut from 40 minutes to 30 minutes. And five courses—art, music/choir, foreign language, technology, and physical education—have had their time allotments slashed!

2   Right now, I have six class periods throughout the day. The morning bell rings at 7:50 a.m. and the day closes with the final bell at 3:00 p.m. Each class runs for 60 minutes, and we have five minutes to change classes. There is also a 40-minute lunch break. This schedule gives a nice range of subjects. I am not stressed out about getting to class on time, and I am able to enjoy a nice lunch halfway through the day.

3   Under the new schedule, the bell will still ring at 7:50 a.m., but our first four class times will stretch for 85 minutes. The time between classes also has been decreased. Five minutes of hall travel has been pushed down to 180 seconds. The last class each day—fifth period—will offer the reduced-time courses I mentioned previously. These teachers will only have 45 minutes to educate students.

4   Periods one through four will offer English Language Arts, Science, Social Studies, and Math. Your fifth period subject is optional. Since these classes are given on either Monday, Wednesday, and Friday, or Tuesday and Thursday, you can select two of the courses offered. As I said before, no study hall periods are allowed. Teachers are permitted to offer 15-minute study intervals in the first four periods.

Go On ►

---

4.   The author probably wrote this passage to—

    A. show the difference between archaeology and anthropology.

    ✗ B. explain the importance of anthropology and archaeology.

    C. entertain readers with a story about lost civilizations.

    D. persuade readers to become archaeologists.

5.   Which of the following professionals would be the **best** choice to call to determine the importance of a farmer's collection of arrowheads and stone tools found during 30 years of farming her land?

    A. a physical anthropologist, because she or he could determine the physical characteristics of a person who would use such tools

    ✗ B. an archaeologist, because she or he could determine the ages of the tools and also determine which people might have used them

    C. a police officer, because she or he would know the history of the area and could determine who had farmed the land in years past

    D. a cultural anthropologist, because she or he would be able to give a monetary value to the tools

Go On ►

5   The problems with the new schedule are obvious. While I agree core subjects such as Math and Science are important, I don't think extended periods of study should be implemented at the expense of other classes. Artists and musicians should not be deprived of valuable learning experiences; neither should those interested in technology, foreign languages, and sports. These courses are important building blocks for high school. Does the school board want to foster unprepared students? High school classes are more varied, and require completion of a wide variety of subjects. Without a good foundation, eighth graders will face many difficulties.

6   In addition to fewer course offerings, we face a shorter amount of time between classes. I am expected to travel four flights of stairs, to maneuver my way through halls full of people, and to walk from the east side of the building to the west wing in 180 seconds. This is nearly impossible. I would like to see a school board member attempt this feat; I don't think our five-minute break should change.

7   Finally, I am disappointed by the reduced lunch period. Thirty minutes is hardly enough time for students to get through the lunch line; some students wait almost 20 minutes just to get their food trays. That leaves 10 minutes to find a seat in the very crowded cafeteria and to eat. My stomach hurts thinking about trying to rush through a meal so fast.

8   As you can see, the new school schedule is really going to shake things up at Upper Valley. I hope the school board will reconsider its decision. The new schedule doesn't help students; it negatively impacts them, and I think more student input is necessary. I would be happy to represent the student body if a hearing to review the new schedule is offered.

9   Sincerely,
Van Kokowski

Go On

---

6. Van Kokowski's viewpoint on the proposed school schedule change is—

   A. proactive.

   X B. negative.

   C. unconcerned.

   D. undecided.

7. How has the author organized the second half of this letter?

   X A. The author listed arguments and supported each argument with personal opinions.

   B. The author listed arguments and supported each argument with factual research.

   C. The author listed facts about the new schedule and did not include personal opinions.

   D. The author did not list facts about the new schedule but did include personal opinions.

8. The primary reason most students will oppose this new schedule change is because—

   A. the number of classes has been reduced from six to five.

   X B. the five-minute class change time is reduced.

   C. there are fewer course offerings during the day.

   D. no study hall periods are allowed during the day.

Go On

Read this selection. Then answer the questions that follow.

The Raven

by Edgar Allan Poe

1   Once upon a midnight dreary, while I pondered, weak and weary,
    Over many a quaint and curious volume of forgotten lore,
    While I nodded, nearly napping, suddenly there came a tapping,
    As of some one gently rapping, rapping at my chamber door.
    " 'Tis some visitor," I muttered, "tapping at my chamber door-
    Only this, and nothing more."

2   Ah, distinctly I remember it was in the bleak December,
    And each separate dying ember wrought its ghost upon the floor.
    Eagerly I wished the morrow:—vainly I had sought to borrow
    From my books surcease[1] of sorrow—sorrow for the lost Lenore—
    For the rare and radiant maiden whom the angels name Lenore—
    Nameless here for evermore.

3   And the silken sad uncertain rustling of each purple curtain
    Thrilled me—filled me with fantastic terrors never felt before;
    So that now, to still the beating of my heart, I stood repeating,
    " 'Tis some visitor entreating entrance at my chamber door—
    Some late visitor entreating entrance at my chamber door;—
    This it is, and nothing more."

4   Presently my soul grew stronger; hesitating then no longer,
    "Sir," said I, "or Madam, truly your forgiveness I implore;
    But the fact is I was napping, and so gently you came rapping,
    And so faintly you came tapping, tapping at my chamber door,
    That I scarce was sure I heard you"—here I opened wide the door;—
    Darkness there, and nothing more.

[1] surcease: an end

---

9. Read this sentence.

    "And five courses—art, music/choir, foreign language, technology, and physical
    education—have had their time *allotments* slashed!"

    What does the word *allotment* mean?

    A. performance

    ✗ B. portion

    C. pleasing

    D. pretty

10. Which of the following is an opinion statement made by the author?

    A. "As I said before, no study hall periods are allowed."

    ✗ B. "Thirty minutes is hardly enough time for students to get through the lunch line."

    C. "Under the new schedule, the bell will still ring at 7:50 a.m., but our first four class times
       will stretch for 85 minutes."

    D. "The decision reduced the number of class periods each day from six to five."

Show What You Know® on the Common Core for Grade 8 Reading

5   Deep into that darkness peering, long I stood there wondering, fearing,
Doubting, dreaming dreams no mortals ever dared to dream before;
But the silence was unbroken, and the stillness gave no token,
And the only word there spoken was the whispered word, "Lenore!"
This I whispered, and an echo murmured back the word, "Lenore!"—
Merely this, and nothing more.

6   Back into the chamber turning, all my soul within me burning,
Soon again I heard a tapping somewhat louder than before.
"Surely," said I, "surely that is something at my window lattice:
Let me see, then, what thereat[2] is, and this mystery explore—
Let my heart be still a moment and this mystery explore;—
'Tis the wind and nothing more."

7   Open here I flung the shutter, when, with many a flirt and flutter,
In there stepped a stately raven of the saintly days of yore;
Not the least obeisance[3] made he; not a minute stopped or stayed he;
But, with mien[4] of lord or lady, perched above my chamber door—
Perched upon a bust of Pallas[5] just above my chamber door—
Perched, and sat, and nothing more.

8   Then this ebony bird beguiling my sad fancy into smiling,
By the grave and stern decorum of the countenance it wore,
"Though thy crest be shorn and shaven, thou," I said, "art sure no craven[6],
Ghastly grim and ancient raven wandering from the Nightly shore—
Tell me what thy lordly name is on the Night's Plutonian shore!"
Quoth the Raven, "Nevermore."

[2] thereat: at theat place
[3] obeisance: a gesture of respect or deference
[4] mien: appearance
[5] Pallas: Greek goddess of wisdom
[6] craven: a coward

9   Much I marvelled this ungainly fowl to hear discourse so plainly,
Though its answer little meaning—little relevancy bore;
For we cannot help agreeing that no living human being
Ever yet was blest with seeing bird above his chamber door—
Bird or beast upon the sculptured bust above his chamber door,
With such name as "Nevermore."

10   But the raven, sitting lonely on the placid bust, spoke only
That one word, as if his soul in that one word he did outpour.
Nothing further then he uttered—not a feather then he fluttered—
Till I scarcely more than muttered, "other friends have flown before—
On the morrow he will leave me, as my hopes have flown before."
Then the bird said, "Nevermore."

11. What conclusion can you draw about the meaning of the poem?

A. The narrator lost his raven that flew back to him.

B. The narrator searches for what is tapping on his chamber door.

X C. The narrator lost a woman he loved named Lenore and the raven is now his solemn companion.

D. The narrator loves Lenore and the raven.

12. In paragraph 1 of the poem, why does the author include the alliteration of "while," "weak," and "weary"?

X A. to set up the rhythm of the poem

B. to show the reader how active the narrator is

C. to move the poem along at a fast pace

D. to require the reader to read the poem aloud

13. How does the narrator's mood change when he sees the raven?

A. The narrator is peacefully reading then the raven comes in and scares him.

X B. At first, the narrator is afraid; then he is happy the raven chose to come into his chamber and give him company.

C. The narrator is afraid then he sees the raven and feels remorse.

D. The narrator is happy then the raven comes in and scares him.

14. Which sentence **best** summarizes of the poem?

A. The narrator was sad and tired one night, and was startled when Lenore knocked on the door.

X B. The narrator was depressed over losing his love, and he has to live the rest of his life with the raven in his house.

C. The narrator was tired one night and dreamt of a talking bird.

D. The narrator was depressed over losing his love, who appeared to him in the form of a raven.

15. In your own words, explain how the poet's use of repetition is effective in developing the meaning of the poem.

Support your answer with details from the poem.

Poe uses repetition to help show that the poet has lost his true love and will not see her again. He repeats the words "Lenore" and "nevermore" to make his point. He also uses repetition to add suspense to the poem.

Read this selection. Then answer the questions that follow.

Faces on the Mount

History of Mount Rushmore

1   Around 1923, South Dakota's state historians were looking to attract visitors to the area. A suggestion was made to carve a giant statue in the Black Hills.

2   Gutzon Borglum, a well-respected sculptor of the time known for his artistic celebration of all things American, was commissioned for the project in 1925. Born in Idaho, the son of Danish Mormons, Borglum studied art in Paris. He made a name for himself on projects including remodeling the Statue of Liberty's torch and working on an oversized Lincoln bust for the U.S. Capitol. Borglum scoured the Black Hills for a location suitable to his plans and settled on Mount Rushmore, named for New York lawyer Charles E. Rushmore in 1885. The site consisted of a broad wall of exposed granite, which basked in sunlight most of the day.

3   According to Borglum, his vision for Mount Rushmore was "a formal rendering of the philosophy of our government into granite on a mountain peak." His plans grouped together four individuals who led the United States from colonial times through the 20th century: George Washington, Thomas Jefferson, Theodore Roosevelt, and Abraham Lincoln (carved left to right as listed), four of America's most honored presidents.

4   Commencement on the project began in 1927 with a dedication by President Calvin Coolidge, and work took nearly 14 years to complete. Interesting to note, only six and one-half years were actually spent carving the massive structure. Money stood as the biggest obstacle, primarily in the era of the Great Depression. The final cost: nearly $1,000,000.

5   Borglum was the project's biggest advocate. In search of funding for the memorial, he lobbied state officials, Congress, cabinet members, and presidents. He often commented that the masterpiece was far more than a tourist attraction; he referred to it as a "shrine of democracy."

6   Washington's face on the mountain was dedicated in 1930, followed by Jefferson in 1936. The sculpting of Lincoln's face ended in 1937, and the completed face of Roosevelt stood by 1939, although further carving continued until October 1941. Upon Borglum's death in March 1941, the later work was supervised by Borglum's son, Lincoln.

Go On

How Did They Do That?

1   Not only did Borglum envision the amazing monument, he came up with a way to make his concept a reality. Initially, Borglum developed small plaster models using paintings, photographs, descriptions, and his own artistic interpretation. He transferred his work onto the mountain face using a pointing machine. The plaster model of each head was sized by a ratio of one inch to one foot. The models were each fitted with a pointing machine. Borglum's device is described in the next paragraph.

2   A metal shaft (1) was placed upright at the center of each president's head. A protractor plate measuring degrees (2) was positioned at the base of the metal shaft. A horizontal bar (3) hinged at the base of the metal shaft, pivoted across the protractor plate to measure the angle from the central axis. A weighted plumb line (4) hung from the horizontal bar; it slid back and forth, measuring the distance from the central head point. It also was raised and lowered to measure vertical distance from the top of the head. To transfer the model to the mountain, each point was multiplied by 12; each angle measurement remained unchanged. A large-scale pointing machine was anchored at the top of the mountain, and workers used the modified points to start construction on the 60-feet tall faces, which stand nearly 500 feet above the ground.

3   Artisans were not able to add material to the natural face of the mountain, so the only technique available was the careful removal of stone. Being that granite is such a hard material, early work called for the use of explosives to remove large portions of rock. Once Borglum was satisfied with the egg-shaped working surface, the pointing machine was secured. The points measured facial features. As each head became a more defined reality, Borglum studied the large-scale face and made alterations. Then, each facial feature was carefully shaped by workers using simple tools: hammers, wedges, steel drill bits, and air-powered hammers. Their attention to detail adds to the humanity of each figure.

Go On

---

16. What detail given in the article caused the Mount Rushmore project to be delayed?

A. a lack of skilled laborers

X B. a lack of funds

C. protests by environmental groups

D. stormy weather

17. What is the main **difference** between "History of Mount Rushmore" and "How Did They Do That?"

A. "History of Mount Rushmore" is about the process that was used to build Mount Rushmore; "How Did They Do That?" is about Mount Rushmore's development.

B. "History of Mount Rushmore" is a biography of the presidents represented on Mount Rushmore; "How Did They Do That?" is about the process that was used to build Mount Rushmore.

X C. "History of Mount Rushmore" is about the philosophy behind the creation of Mount Rushmore; "How Did They Do That?" is about the process that was used to build Mount Rushmore.

D. "History of Mount Rushmore" is about the process that was used to build Mount Rushmore; "How Did They Do That?" describes the tools used to carve Mount Rushmore.

Go On

18. Which event happened first in the selections "History of Mount Rushmore" and "How Did They Do That?"

A. Washington's face was dedicated.

X B. Borglum developed small plaster models.

C. Work on the monument was supervised by Borglum's son.

D. Borglum used the pointing machine.

19. What does the article mean by saying that Mount Rushmore, "basked in sunlight most of the day,"?

A. Mount Rushmore was hidden from the light of the sun throughout the day.

B. Mount Rushmore blocked sunlight from reaching the Black Hills throughout the day.

X C. Mount Rushmore was touched by sunlight throughout the day.

D. Mount Rushmore reflected sunlight.

20. The author probably wrote "History of Mount Rushmore" to—

A. convince readers to visit Mount Rushmore.

X B. explain the process of creating the faces on Mount Rushmore.

C. tell a story about the life of Gutzon Borglum.

D. describe the sculptures at Mount Rushmore.

21. According to the article, what effect did the sculptors' carefully shaped facial features add to Mount Rushmore?

A. They polished the granite.

B. They preserved the life of each face.

C. They made each face distinguishable.

X D. They brought humanity to each face.

Go On

Right page (Student Workbook 47)

Read this selection. Then answer the questions that follow.

The Scavenger Hunt

Lou's Hunt

1. It was the day of the big scavenger hunt—I was so excited. Our team of four was ready. My teammates had participated in other hunts, but this was my first.

2. I knew their experience would be a great benefit; I was glad they chose me as their fourth member. Charles, Orlando, Sunny, and I met an hour before the start time. The guys plotted a strategy. I took my cues and listened for instructions. I didn't want to let them down. As the minutes clicked by, we were anxious for our first clue.

3. I perused the scavenger hunt instruction sheet. Altogether, there were 15 clues. That seemed like a lot to me, but Orlando assured me the hunt would fly by. I got excited when I reached the bottom of the sheet. It said the 15th clue would reveal the prize. I looked at the other teams around us. They, too, were studying the instructions.

4. As the start time approached, a tall man handed each team a large, white envelope labeled "DO NOT OPEN UNTIL THE BELL RINGS." The envelope carried our first clue. Everyone was anxious to investigate the tip. Orlando was poised to tear open the seal. The bell sounded at 3:00 p.m. Team members feverishly exposed the clue; it read:

5. *You'll recognize the street; it rhymes with the word "rake." Now all you have to do is look for a number that matches Joseph's cake.*

6. "Oh, that's easy!" exclaimed Sunny. "Joe turned 14 last week. His cake had 14 candles. We've got to get to 14 Lake Street."

7. I didn't want to admit I had no idea where 14 Lake Street was, so I hopped on my bike and easily let myself fall to the back of the pack. The guys were in such a hurry; they didn't seem to notice or to mind.

Go On

Left page (Student Workbook 46)

22. What is the purpose of the section titled, "How Did They Do That?"

A. to offer information on how money was raised for the monument

B. to give details on the number of people involved in the 14-year project

C. to show that Gutzon was a talented engineer, but not a talented artist

X D. to show that Gutzon's contribution to the project extended beyond his artistic vision

23. What does Borglum mean when he says his vision for Mount Rushmore was "a formal rendering of the philosophy of our government into granite on a mountain peak"?

X A. The monument stands for leaders who are dedicated to America's democratic principles.

B. The monument was built to honor famous sculptors.

C. The monument was built solely to attract tourists to South Dakota.

D. The monument stands as a memorial to Danish immigrants.

24. Which event happened last in the selections "History of Mount Rushmore" and "How Did They Do That?"

A. Washington's face was dedicated.

B. Borglum developed small plaster models.

X C. Work on the monument was supervised by Borglum's son.

D. Borglum used the pointing machine.

Go On

Show What You Know® on the Common Core for Grade 8 Reading

Orlando's Hunt

13 It was the day of the big scavenger hunt—I was beyond excited. Charles, Sunny, and I have done this before. But Lou, he's new. I was hoping he wouldn't slow us down. We won this hunt last year, and we have a title to defend. I wanted to plot a strategy, so I suggested we meet an hour before the start time. I gave Lou a few pointers. He nodded in agreement; I was pretty sure he didn't understand. I worried about this guy. He blankly stared at the scavenger hunt instruction sheet—no expression. "A fish out of water," I thought to myself. I hoped something was sinking in.

14 The other teams were watching us. They knew they had to beat us to win. When the first clue was distributed, I held it tightly in my hand. At the sound of the bell, I tore into it.

15 "Looks like we're going to 14 Lake Street," Sunny figured out the clue.

16 I steered my bike toward Blake Alley—a little short cut I've been taking on my way home from school. Lou had a hard time keeping up. We couldn't leave him. All four team members had to complete the hunt. Sunny and Charles stopped so he could make up the distance. I slowed my pace, but kept moving down the alley. "Let's go, let's go."

17 I spotted Mrs. Hoster, ditched my bike in her front yard, and rushed up to the porch. She handed me a green balloon. I could see the clue tucked inside. I jumped from the porch to pop the balloon. My team finally made it to 14 Lake Street, but I was thinking of our next destination: Golden Park.

14 Lake Street

18 The guys followed me. Lou was doing a little better at keeping pace, but I knew his slow down in the alley hurt us. The basket of clues under a tree in Golden Park greeted a few teams before us. I read the clue as my teammates rounded the bike path.

19 "Don't slow down. I'll meet you there. I dropped my house key in the basket. I have to get it." I grabbed my house key and shoved a couple clues in my pocket. "We're not going to lose."

---

8 "Let's take Blake Alley. We'll cut over to Hedges Drive; it intersects with Lake."

9 Sounded like a good idea to me. Orlando took off for the journey without discussion. He led us through the "short cut." I pedaled to keep up. Unfamiliar with the area, I didn't realize Blake Alley was taking us several minutes longer than anticipated. Charles knew it. But it was too late to back track or to argue. Our approach to Lake Street offered glimpses of several teams on the front porch of 14 Lake Street.

10 Mrs. Hoster, my English teacher, gently rocked back and forth on 14 Lake Street's old porch swing. Orlando felt bad about the delay and rushed to seize the next clue. She handed him a green balloon. Puzzled, he decided to forgo the steps and jumped to the sidewalk. The balloon slipped from his grasp and popped as it encountered the ground. A tightly folded paper was revealed. The three of us couldn't wait to see what it said.

11 *Up the ladder, down the slide, round and round on a colorful ride. Look around this playful place, you'll be one step closer to the end of the race.*

12 Our next trek took us to Golden Park, where a displaced basket—filled with brown paper sacks—rested under a tree. Teams were coming and going. Orlando grabbed our clue. The rest of us kept on riding, barely slowing down. He shouted the clue and told us he'd meet us there. "I dropped my house key in the basket. I have to get it."

Left Panel

25. Read the sentence from the selection "Lou's Hunt."

"Team members *feverishly* exposed the clue; it read:

You'll recognize the street; it rhymes with the word "rake." Now all you have to do is look for a number that matches Joseph's cake."

What does the word *feverishly* mean?

X A. with excitement

B. in the heat

C. with anger

D. with fear

26. Why was Lou excited about the scavenger hunt?

A. He was really good at scavenger hunts.

X B. It was his first scavenger hunt.

C. He knew the answer to the first clue.

D. His team had always won in the past.

Go On

Right Panel

27. The author organizes this story by—

A. explaining how a scavenger hunt works.

B. comparing and contrasting this year's scavenger hunt to last year's scavenger hunt.

X C. describing a scavenger hunt from different perspectives.

D. describing the best way to approach a scavenger hunt.

28. Which sentence from this story supports the idea that Orlando is the leader of the group?

A. "That seemed like a lot to me, but Orlando assured me the hunt would fly by."

B. "Orlando was poised to tear open the seal."

X C. "Orlando took off for the journey without discussion."

D. "Unfamiliar with the area, I didn't realize Blake Alley was taking us several minutes longer than anticipated."

29. Paragraph 7 of "Lou's Hunt" is important to this story because it—

A. shows that Lou is inexperienced in scavenger hunts.

X B. explains why Lou's group fell behind in the scavenger hunt.

C. describes the shortcut the boys took during the scavenger hunt.

D. tells why the other team members trust Orlando's shortcut.

30. Read this sentence from "Orlando's Hunt."

"A fish out of water," I thought to myself.

What does Orlando mean by this?

X A. Lou is out of place at the scavenger hunt.

B. Orlando is glad to have Lou on his team.

C. Lou is too slow to keep up with the team.

D. Lou has participated in many scavenger hunts.

Go On

34. What is a major idea found in both "Lou's Hunt" and "Orlando's Hunt"?

✗ A. wanting to win the scavenger hunt

B. cheating to get ahead

C. desiring to fit in with the group

D. trusting others

35. What is one difference between "Lou's Hunt" and "Orlando's Hunt"?

A. Orlando's story is about cheating to win the scavenger hunt, but Lou's story is about winning the scavenger hunt fairly.

✗ B. Lou's story is about following someone else's lead, but Orlando's story is about taking the lead.

C. Orlando's story is about winning the scavenger hunt, but Lou's story is not.

D. Lou's story is about making plans to go on a scavenger hunt, but Orlando's story is about actually going on the scavenger hunt.

Go On

---

31. The reader can conclude that Orlando shoved a couple of clues in his pocket because he—

A. accidentally grabbed them with his house key.

✗ B. wanted to prevent other teams from getting the clues.

C. wanted to show them to his teammates.

D. thought it would help them catch up with the other teams.

32. How is Lou's interpretation of the scavenger hunt different from Orlando's version of the experience?

Use details from the story to support your response.

33. Because "Lou's Hunt" and "Orlando's Hunt" are told from the author's point of view, the reader can—

A. comprehend the feelings of each player on the team.

B. realize what it is like to go on a scavenger hunt.

C. tell that winning a scavenger hunt is hard work.

✗ D. understand each author's feelings about the scavenger hunt.

Lou has never been on a scavenger hunt before. Orlando has not only participated, but he won the hunt the year prior. From the start, both boys have different perspectives. Orlando is confident, commenting the other teams are watching his team's strategy. Lou is nervous and carefully studies the instructions. Another major difference in the stories comes when the boys head for the second clue on Lake Street. According to Lou, Sunny and Charles think this route is out of the way and if slows them down. Orlando has a different version: Lou can't keep up with the team and he slows them down. In finding the second clue, Orlando says he popped the balloon because he knew a clue was inside. Lou, however, says finding the clue was an accident.

Go On

10   José looked around the room. "There had better not be any questions," he murmured. "Let's not drag this out any longer than it has to be."

11   Mr. Garcia set up his laptop computer. The laptop was connected to a device that projected the computer screen's image onto the wall—a colorful building came into focus. The building's blue-green windows reflected the sky, and its unusual shape reminded José of a mountain or a pyramid. "If you're wondering how this magnificent building came to be, you might enjoy architecture," Mr. Garcia began.

12   José sat up in his seat. His gruffness faded as the architect continued. José gazed at blueprints, sketches, angles, pictures of scale models, close-ups of windows and doors, and more photographs of buildings. "I can do this," he thought in silence. "It's like I've been telling Mrs. Radcliffe all along: who needs English class? Why read old books and long poems, when there are drafting projects to complete? I'm going to be an architect."

13   José was fascinated. Pictures of modern buildings with clean lines and geometric shapes captured his imagination. He focused on their structures and on the types of materials used for construction—wood, steel, glass, and stone. José was so busy looking at the buildings he didn't hear Mr. Garcia mention becoming an architect was no easy task. "This profession is hard work, as are many others. If you want to be an architect, start studying now. In order to be accepted into a collegiate architecture program, you need to get good grades in high school. Education requirements include at least five years of college classes from a wide variety of disciplines as well as a stint as an architectural apprentice."

14   As the presentation wrapped, José's arm reached into the air.

15   "Mr. Garcia, I want to ask a question."

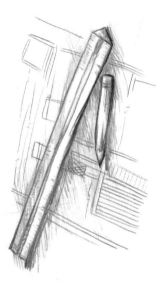

Read this selection. Then answer the questions that follow.

Class Project

1   José entered the classroom, threw his backpack on the floor, and slumped into his desk with a loud sigh. "Prepare for boredom," he announced to the few classmates who were already in the room.

2   José had been dreading this day. A few weeks prior, Mrs. Radcliffe announced the career project. Her eighth-grade English students would explore a possible career choice.

3   Research requirements included speaking with someone in the chosen field, identifying education prerequisites and the availability of current job postings, and writing up a description of career duties. The announcement did not sit well with José. "Another research paper," he grumbled to himself. "I don't know what I want to do with my life. I'm only fourteen!" Similar groans echoed about his classmates.

4   José was not looking forward to hearing from Mrs. Radcliffe's guests. Each planned to speak about his or her personal career experiences and had prepared information on his or her respective career topic. An entire morning of adults talking about themselves, he couldn't think of anything more boring. "I've got this great drafting project I'm working on, and I can't wait to get back to it. Do you think she'd notice if we ditched the speakers and headed to the computer lab?" José asked his friend Marita.

5   "She'll notice." She assured him. José considered an appeal, but he knew she was right.

6   Mrs. Radcliffe hushed the class and began her explanation. "I know many of you feel as though eighth grade is too early to starting thinking about a career, but I want to assure you it's not. You'll be heading off to high school next year, and you're going to have many choices to make. I hope this project will help you explore your options. Now, I would like to introduce our five speakers."

7   "I should have brought a pillow," José thought. "I could have used this time for a nap."

8   Mrs. Radcliffe introduced each speaker. José stared at each individual, confident he would learn nothing. There was a banker, then a magazine editor, a doctor, an auto mechanic….

9   "… and last, but not least, please welcome Rudy Garcia. Mr. Garcia is an architect with the firm Garcia Partners Design. He has an appointment today, so I've asked him to present first. Mr. Garcia said he will be happy to answer your questions, but please hold your questions until the end of his presentation. If you don't think you'll be able to remember, write them down."

---

38. Read the sentence from the selection.

"Research requirements included speaking with someone in the chosen field, identifying education *prerequisites* and the availability of current job postings, and writing up a description of career duties."

What does the word *prerequisites* mean?

   A. knowledge

✗**B.** requirements

   C. courses

   D. elements

39. Which of the following statements **best** summarizes this story?

   A. Jose has a bad attitude about working on the class project.

✗**B.** Through a school assignment he does not want to do, Jose discovers a career he is interested in.

   C. Mr. Garcia addresses the eighth graders, because he wants to change Jose's feelings toward his future.

   D. Mrs. Radcliffe assigns a class project about future careers.

---

36. In your own words, write a summary of "Class Project."

Support your answer with details from the selection.

José comes to class not looking forward to hearing the guest speakers on career day. He wants to work on a project of his own. Much to his surprise, José realizes that he can learn a lot from one of the guest speakers, who happens to be an architect.

37. How are Mrs. Radcliffe and Mr. Garcia **similar**?

   A. They both are disappointed with Jose's attitude toward the career project.

   B. They both went to school for five years.

   C. They both like architecture.

✗**D.** They both stress that eighth graders should start thinking about their futures.

Assessment One

40. José's attitude can best be described as—

A. serious.

X **B.** sarcastic.

C. determined.

D. animated.

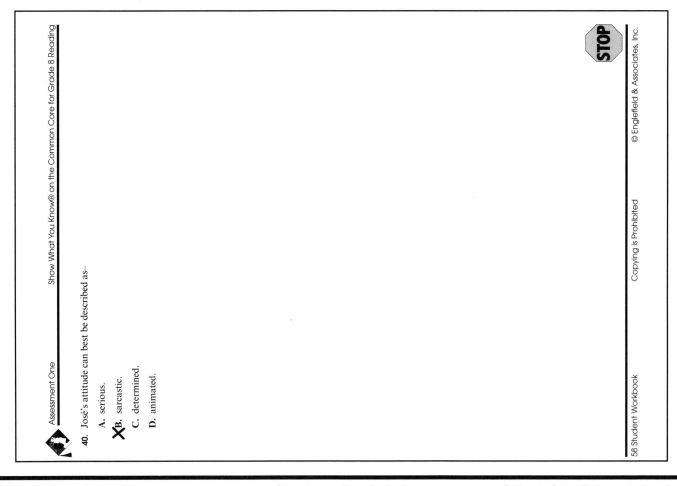

1 ● Ⓑ Ⓒ Ⓓ

2 Ⓐ Ⓑ ● Ⓓ

3 ● Ⓑ Ⓒ Ⓓ

4 Ⓐ ● Ⓒ Ⓓ

5 Ⓐ ● Ⓒ Ⓓ

6 Ⓐ ● Ⓒ Ⓓ

7 ● Ⓑ Ⓒ Ⓓ

8 Ⓐ ● Ⓒ Ⓓ

9 Ⓐ ● Ⓒ Ⓓ

10 Ⓐ ● Ⓒ Ⓓ

11 Ⓐ Ⓑ ● Ⓓ

12 ● Ⓑ Ⓒ Ⓓ

13 Ⓐ ● Ⓒ Ⓓ

14 Ⓐ ● Ⓒ Ⓓ

15

Poe uses repetition to help show that the poet has lost his true love and will not see her again. He repeats the words "Lenore" and "nevermore" to make his point. He also uses repetition to add suspense to the poem.

16 Ⓐ ● Ⓒ Ⓓ

17 Ⓐ Ⓑ ● Ⓓ

18 Ⓐ ● Ⓒ Ⓓ

19 Ⓐ Ⓑ ● Ⓓ

20 Ⓐ ● Ⓒ Ⓓ

21 Ⓐ Ⓑ Ⓒ ●

22 Ⓐ Ⓑ Ⓒ ●

23 ● Ⓑ Ⓒ Ⓓ

24 Ⓐ Ⓑ ● Ⓓ

25 ● Ⓑ Ⓒ Ⓓ

26 Ⓐ ● Ⓒ Ⓓ

27 Ⓐ Ⓑ ● Ⓓ

28 Ⓐ Ⓑ ● Ⓓ

29 Ⓐ ● Ⓒ Ⓓ

30 ● Ⓑ Ⓒ Ⓓ

31 Ⓐ ● Ⓒ Ⓓ

32

> Lou has never been on a scavenger hunt before. Orlando has not
> only participated, but he won the hunt the year prior. From the
> start, both boys have different perspectives. Orlando is confident,
> commenting the other teams are watching his team's strategy.
> Lou is nervous and carefully studies the instructions. Another major
> difference in the stories comes when the boys head for the second
> clue on Lake Street. According to Lou, Sunny and Charles think this
> route is out of the way and it slows them down. Orlando has a
> different version: Lou can't keep up with the team and he slows
> them down. In finding the second clue, Orlando says he popped
> the balloon because he knew a clue was inside. Lou, however,
> says finding the clue was an accident.

33 Ⓐ Ⓑ Ⓒ ●

34 ● Ⓑ Ⓒ Ⓓ

35 Ⓐ ● Ⓒ Ⓓ

36

> José comes to class not looking forward to hearing the guest speakers on career day. He wants to work on a project of his own. Much to his surprise, José realizes that he can learn a lot from one of the guest speakers, who happens to be an architect.

37 Ⓐ Ⓑ Ⓒ ●

38 Ⓐ ● Ⓒ Ⓓ

39 Ⓐ ● Ⓒ Ⓓ

40 Ⓐ ● Ⓒ Ⓓ

Question	Standard	Answer	Keywords
1	RI.8.6	A	Author's Purpose
2	RI.8.2	C	Main Idea
3	RI.8.4	A	Use Context Clues
4	RI.8.6	B	Author's Purpose
5	RI.8.3	B	Analyze Text
6	RI.8.6	B	Author's Purpose
7	RI.8.5	A	Main Idea
8	RI.8.1	B	Make Inferences
9	RI.8.4	B	Definition
10	RI.8.8	B	Fact and Opinion
11	RL.8.1	C	Draw Conclusions
12	RL.8.4	A	Literary Device, Alliteration
13	RL.8.4	B	Character Development
14	RL.8.2	B	Summary
15	RL.8.3	—	Literary Terminology
16	RI.8.3	B	Cause and Effect
17	RI.8.9	C	Compare and Contrast
18	RI.8.3	B	Sequences
19	RI.8.4	C	Analyze Words
20	RI.8.6	B	Author's Purpose

—see analysis for constructed response

Question	Standard	Answer	Keywords
21	RI.8.1	D	Cause and Effect
22	RI.8.6	D	Purpose
23	RI.8.1	A	Inferences
24	RI.8.3	C	Sequences
25	RL.8.4	A	Bring Meanings to Words in Context
26	RL.8.1	B	Cite Textual Evidence
27	RL.8.5	C	Compare and Contrast
28	RL.8.1	C	Support Responses
29	RL.8.3	B	Plot
30	RL.8.4	A	Literary Devices
31	RL.8.1	B	Draw Conclusions
32	RL.8.5	—	Compare and Contrast
33	RL.8.6	D	Author's Point of View
34	RL.8.5	A	Compare Ideas Across Text
35	RL.8.5	B	Find Differences Across Text
36	RL.8.2	—	Summary
37	RL.8.2	D	Determine Theme
38	RL.8.4	B	Define Words
39	RL.8.2	B	Summary
40	RL.8.6	B	Point of View

—see analysis for constructed response

Reading Assessment One: Correlation Chart

Use this chart to identify areas for improvement for individual students or for the class as a whole. For example, enter students' names in the left-hand column. When a student misses a question, place an "X" in the corresponding box. A column with a large number of "Xs" shows that the class needs more practice with that particular objective.

Correlation	RI.8.6	RI.8.2	RI.8.4	RI.8.6	RI.8.3	RI.8.6	RI.8.5	RI.8.1	RI.8.4	RI.8.8	RI.8.1	RL.8.4	RI.8.4	RL.8.2	RL.8.3	RI.8.3	RI.8.9	RI.8.3	RI.8.4	RI.8.6
Answer	A	C	A	B	B	B	A	B	B	B	C	A	B	B	—	B	C	B	C	B
Question	1	2	3	4	5	6	7	8	9	10	11	12	13	14	15	16	17	18	19	20

Student Names

—see analysis for constructed response

Reading Assessment One: Correlation Chart

Correlation	RI.8.1	RI.8.6	RI.8.1	RI.8.3	RI.8.4	RL.8.1	RL.8.5	RL.8.1	RL.8.3	RL.8.4	RL.8.1	RL.8.5	RL.8.6	RL.8.5	RL.8.5	RL.8.2	RL.8.2	RL.8.4	RL.8.2	RL.8.6
Answer	D	D	A	C	A	B	C	C	B	A	B	—	D	A	B	—	D	B	B	B
Question	21	22	23	24	25	26	27	28	29	30	31	32	33	34	35	36	37	38	39	40

Student Names

—*see analysis for constructed response*

Reading Assessment Two

Responses *Throughout this section, pages from Reading Assessment Two of the Student Workbook are included in reduced-page format. Correct multiple-choice answers and sample responses for each constructed-response item are indicated.*

Reading Assessment Two

Directions for Taking the Reading Assessment

The Reading Assessment contains eight reading selections and 40 questions. Some of the selections are fiction, while others are nonfiction. Read each selection and the questions that follow carefully. You may look back at any selection as many times as you would like. If you are unsure of a question, you can move to the next question, and go back to the question you skipped later.

Multiple-choice questions require you to pick the best answer out of four possible choices. Only one answer is correct. The short-answer questions will ask you to write your answer and explain your thinking using words. Remember to read the questions and the answer choices carefully. You will mark your answers on the answer document.

When you finish, check your answers.

Student Workbook 63

Directions:

This Grade 8 Reading Assessment has multiple-choice and short-answer questions.

There are several important things to remember as you take this test:

- Read each multiple-choice question carefully. Think about what is being asked. Then fill in one answer bubble to mark your answer.

- If you do not know the answer to a multiple-choice question, skip it and go on. If you have time, go back to the questions you skipped and answer them.

- For short-answer questions, write your response clearly and neatly in the box provided.

- If you finish the Assessment early, go back and check over your work.

The Wise Judge

Read this selection. Then answer the questions that follow.

1   Long ago in the Chinese countryside lived a man named Chang Fu-Yen, a farmer who lived off the money he raised by selling his crops. He earned a nice sum by selling the garlic he grew. During a drought one summer, the farmer struggled to grow his garlic. Knowing that if his crop died or was stolen by a robber, he would be left with nothing, Chang Fu-Yen built a small shack around his garlic. He stayed in the shack night after night to guard his crop. One night the air became chilly, and the farmer left his post for the warmth of his home. The next morning he was shocked to find an empty garden. All the garlic was gone.

2   Because there was no evidence, Chang Fu-Yen could not find the thief on his own. He decided to travel to the city to meet a wise judge with a reputation for solving the most difficult cases. Upon meeting the judge, Chang Fu-Yen was questioned about evidence and witnesses. Because neither existed, the judge ordered the farmer to bring the shack to court for questioning. The judge insisted the shack must have seen something during the robbery. Chang Fu-Yen was confused and the court observers were amused, but the poor man did as he was told.

3   When the shack was brought to the court for questioning, it did not answer the questions asked by the judge. Although it was against the judge's rules, the people in the courtroom howled uncontrollably. After questioning the shack again and still getting no answers, the wise judge ordered the shack to be taken apart, wood slat by wood slat. The observers laughed at the judge. The judge was angered by the laughter, and she punished everyone in the courtroom by fining each observer one pound of garlic.

4   Chang Fu-Yen was very confused by the actions, but he had great confidence in the wise judge's ability. As the garlic was collected, the name of each person who brought garlic was attached to its packet. There were so many people who had been fined, almost all of the garlic in the city had been collected by the judge. The judge then ordered Chang Fu-Yen to go through all the garlic to see if he could find his own garlic. The farmer was able to rule out the older garlic, since his crop had been picked within the past few days. After a few hours of searching, Chang Fu-Yen was able to find his garlic. The thief's name was attached, and the judge ordered the return of all Chang Fu-Yen's garlic.

5   "We have found your garlic," said the wise judge. "We now see who has the last laugh."

Go On ▲

---

1. Why did the judge ask that the shack be brought to her courthouse?

    A. She wanted to prove Chang Fu-Yen was lying.

    B. She wanted the shack to reveal the thief.

    ✗ C. She wanted to trick the observers.

    D. She wanted to test the strength of Chang Fu-Yen's shack.

2. What is the theme of this story?

    A. The law doesn't always make sense.

    B. Fear will force people to confess their wrongdoings.

    ✗ C. You can't hide from your mistakes.

    D. There is no place for humor in a courtroom.

3. What clues in the story give the reader hints about what the judge is planning?

    Use examples, details, and information from the story to support your answer.

    From the title of the story, the reader knows the judge is a wise woman. Since the judge is wise, it is unlikely she would waste her time with a silly request, such as asking the shack to speak. The reader should realize the judge had a greater purpose. It turns out, in this story, she did. She knew asking the shack to talk would make observers laugh. Since laughing in the courtroom was against the rules, the judge fined the people in garlic, so Chang Fu-Yen could find his crop.

Go On ▲

Read this selection. Then answer the questions that follow.

A Wise Judge's Sentence

1   A farmer in ancient China had a neighbor who was a hunter, and who owned ferocious and poorly trained hunting dogs. They jumped the fence frequently and chased the farmer's lambs. The farmer asked his neighbor to keep his dogs in check, but this fell on deaf ears.

2   One day the dogs again jumped the fence and attacked and severely injured several of the lambs.

3   The farmer had had enough, and went to town to consult a judge who listened carefully to the story and said: "I could punish the hunter and instruct him to keep his dogs chained or lock them up. But you would lose a friend and gain an enemy. Which would you rather have, friend or foe for a neighbor?" The farmer replied that he preferred a friend.

4   "Alright, I will offer you a solution that keeps your lambs safe, and which will keep your neighbor a friend." Having heard the judge's solution, the farmer agreed.

5   Once at home, the farmer immediately put the judge's suggestions to the test. He took three of his best lambs and presented them to his neighbor's three small sons, who were beside themselves with joy and began to play with them. To protect his son's newly acquired playthings, the hunter built a strong kennel for his dogs. Since then, the dogs never again bothered the farmer's lambs.

6   Out of gratitude for the farmer's generosity toward his sons, the hunter often shared the game he had hunted with the farmer. The farmer reciprocated by sending the hunter lamb meat and cheese he had made. Within a short time the neighbors became good friends.

---

4. Which of the following sentences has an example of foreshadowing?

  A. "He earned a nice sum by selling the garlic he grew."

✗ B. "Knowing that if his crop died or was stolen by a robber, he would be left with nothing, Chang Fu-Yen built a small shack around his garlic."

  C. "The judge insisted that the shack must have seen something during the robbery."

  D. "There were so many people who had been fined, almost all of the garlic in the city had been collected by the judge."

5. What is most likely the author's purpose for writing "A Wise Judge"?

✗ A. to teach a lesson that everything is not as it seems

  B. to entertain with a story about an eccentric judge

  C. to describe the judicial process

  D. to explain how judges treat witnesses

Read this selection. Then answer the questions that follow.

Early Exploration of Earth's Moon

1   Man has long been interested in the moon. Throughout the years, visual exploration via telescopes and human eyes has peaked curiosity. But, before Americans could actually get to the moon, they had to figure out how to get humans into space.

2   Project Mercury, which ran from 1958 to 1963, was the United States' first man-in-space program. The program endeavored to place a manned spacecraft into space for the purpose of orbiting Earth, to investigate man's ability to function in space, and to return both man and the spacecraft to Earth, safely. America's first manned space flight succeeded when Alan Shepard, Jr., became the first American in space on May 5, 1961. Only a few months prior, the Union of Soviet Socialist Republics (USSR) sent a cosmonaut[1], Yuri Gagarin, into space. At that time, the United States and USSR were involved in what became known as the "space race." The ultimate goal of each nation was to reach the moon. Altogether, the Project Mercury program launched six manned space flights from 1961 to 1963.

3   In late 1961, a plan was announced to send a two-man craft into space. Named the Gemini program in early 1962, this project utilized previous space experiences to build a bigger and better Mercury spacecraft. One goal of the Gemini program included subjecting astronauts to longer space flights; officials knew a trip to the moon would require such. Other objectives involved improving techniques for maneuvering the spacecraft, perfecting methods of spacecraft reentry into Earth's atmosphere, and landing the spacecraft in a pre-determined land location. All goals but the last were achieved before Gemini gave way to the Apollo program by 1967.

[1] cosmonaut: a Russian astronaut

Source: NASA

Go On

---

6.   In paragraph 1 of "A Wise Judge's Sentence," why does the author include figurative language?

X A.   to exaggerate the hunter's lack of response to the farmer's request

B.   to explain that the hunter did not hear the farmer's request

C.   to clarify that the farmer did not ask the hunter for help

D.   to make it clear that the hunter and the farmer did not speak to each other

7.   Which sentence tells how the author feels about kindness?

A.   The author believes it does not pay to be nice.

B.   The author believes you should be nice only after someone has been nice to you.

X C.   The author believes that kindness leads to rewards.

D.   The author believes that kindness will not get you what you want.

8.   How do Chang Fu-Yen's feelings about the judge in "The Wise Judge" compare to the farmer's feelings about the judge in "A Wise Judge's Sentence"?

Include **one** detail from "The Wise Judge" and **one** detail from "A Wise Judge's Sentence" in your answer.

Both Chang Fu-Yen and the farmer trust each judge they go to for help. In "The Wise Judge," Chang Fu-Yen brings the shack to court and takes it apart when the judge asks him to even though he does not understand why. In "A Wise Judge's Sentence," the farmer agrees to follow the judge's advice by giving the hunter's sons each a lamb instead of having the judge punish the hunter.

Go On

Right panel (questions 9–11)

9. What is most likely the author's purpose for writing this selection?

   A. to persuade readers to go to the moon

   B. to explain why the lunar programs didn't work

   C. to tell about the space race between the United States and Russia

   X D. to give information about the exploration of the moon

10. Suppose you are on a committee to decide if space programs should be funded.

    Provide **four** ideas from the selection that could best be used to encourage people to continue to make donations to fund the space program.

    People should continue to make donations to fund the space program because man has always been interested in the moon and stars. Man's exploration of the moon has allowed us to find ways to put humans in space. It has allowed us to create and build new machines on Earth for space travel and space exploration, such as the space shuttle. Space exploration has also allowed us to collect moon rock samples, giving us information on the formation and history of the universe.

11. Which statement best supports the main idea that the Apollo Program was successful in sending humans to the moon?

    A. Astronauts were rigorously trained for the space program.

    B. The United States and USSR were involved in the "space race."

    C. The Apollo Program was designed to send humans to the moon.

    X D. Neil Armstrong was famous for his walk on the moon.

Go On

Left panel (passage)

4   The Apollo program was designed to send humans to the moon. On July 20, 1969, that goal was achieved. Apollo 11 astronaut Neil Armstrong became the first human to walk on the moon. His words echoed throughout the world, "That's one small step for a man, one giant leap for mankind." Five future Apollo missions reached the moon before the program concluded in December 1972. These lunar[2] missions included experiments on the moon's surface conditions. Photographs were taken, and the crew was able to collect surface materials. After thousands of years of speculation, some of the mystery of the moon had finally been solved.

[2] lunar: determined by, relating to, or resembling the moon

Facts About Earth's Moon

- In ancient times, people thought the dark areas on the moon were seas and the lighter areas were continents. Exploration has proven these theories incorrect. No liquid has been found on the moon.

- The diameter of the moon is approximately 2,160 miles (3,480 kilometers), which is about one-fourth of Earth's diameter.

- Scientists believe Earth and the moon are the same age—nearly 4.6 billion years old.

- On the surface of the moon, temperatures range from 260° Fahrenheit (127° Celsius) to −280° Fahrenheit (−173° Celsius).

- The first man-made object to reach the moon was an unmanned Russian spacecraft named Luna 2. It landed on September 14, 1959.

- At any given time, an Earth-bound observer can see no more than 50% of the moon's surface.

- The gravitational pull on the moon is only one-sixth of the pull on Earth.

Go On

12. Which sentence **best** explains why Americans went into space?

✗ A. "Man has long been interested in the moon."

B. "Throughout the years, visual exploration via telescopes and human eyes has peaked curiosity."

C. "The program sought to send a manned spacecraft into space for the purpose of orbiting Earth, to investigate man's ability to function in space, and to return both man and the spacecraft safely to Earth."

D. "The ultimate goal of each nation was to reach the moon."

13. The reader can conclude that astronauts on the moon encounter—

✗ A. natural temperature ranges that are far more extreme than on Earth.

B. large bodies of water.

C. natural temperature ranges that are close to those found on Earth.

D. the same gravitational pull experienced on Earth.

Go On

Read this selection. Then answer the questions that follow.

Early Exploration of Mars

1. Once man uncovered some of the mysteries of the moon, he began to look to other planets in the universe. Among those that held great fascination was Mars. It was known to the first stargazers as the "red star." For ancient civilizations, this red star represented good and evil. The Romans named their god of war after the planet, while others believed the sighting of this planet was an omen of things to come.

2. Today, scientists have determined that Mars is the closest Earth-like planet; this presents the question of whether or not life might be present on the planet. As a result, the exploration of Mars continues to be the focus of missions of the United States, Russia, Japan, and Europe.

3. Since the 1960s, man has attempted to understand this planet by launching unmanned spacecraft to Mars. These exploratory missions are instrumental in gathering data to help scientists answer questions about the planet. The first missions were used to take photographs of the red planet. It was discovered that Mars has volcanoes, but none of them appear to be active. Then orbital missions collected more information. Today, orbiters have landed on Mars to collect further data.

4. It's hard to tell what the future will hold in the exploration of Mars. But one thing is certain. Man will continue to be intrigued by and explore the mysteries of Mars and this universe.

Facts About Mars

- Of all the planets besides Earth, Mars is the only other planet believed capable of supporting life.

- The planet Mars has two moons named Diemos and Phobos.

- Gravity on Mars is less than gravity on Earth.

- A layer of dust called Regolith covers Mars' surface.

- The largest volcano in the Solar System is on Mars.

Go On

The Seminole Tribe of Florida

1   The Seminole Tribe of Florida has a rich history, which dates back approximately 12,000 years. These Native Americans are the descendents of speakers of the Maskoki and Hitchiti languages. The name Seminole is derived from the nickname, cimmaron, meaning free people, given to them by the first Spanish conquerors. The Seminole Tribe's instinct for survival, refusal to be conquered, and drive to remain a free people has allowed them to survive many tumultuous[1] years.

2   Survival in the swamp was always difficult, even in the best circumstances. The River of Grass offered little land to farm, and the Seminoles depended heavily on their fishing and hunting skills to survive. With little shelter from the harsh elements, the Seminoles eventually had to battle, not only the untamed wilderness of the Everglades, but the European settlers as well.

3   The number of Native Americans in Florida has dramatically changed over the years. The most significant changes began in the 1500s when there were approximately 200,000 Native Americans in Florida. However, these numbers significantly decreased after the first European explorers moved into the area. About 80% of the Native-American population in Florida died due to either disease or battles over land. In the 1700s, bands of Creek Indians from Georgia and Alabama began to migrate south to Florida in order to escape conflicts with the Europeans resulting in the first marked increase in population.

4   Over a period of 40 years, the Seminoles fought the U. S. government in order to maintain control over their land. The First Seminole War took place in 1818 and two more major conflicts followed. The third and final Seminole war ended without surrender in 1858 when the United States officially declared an end to the conflict. Although the Seminoles never surrendered, more than 3,000 members of the tribe were forced to move to lands west of the Mississippi River in a mass migration. Only a few hundred members of the tribe were brave enough to stay and battle the elements to remain hidden in the swamps of the Everglades of Florida in defiance of the U. S. government.

[1] tumultuous: violent or overwhelming upheaval

Go On

---

14. In what way are the early missions to the moon and Mars similar?

   A. The missions landed a human on the surface.

   X B. The missions were exploratory in nature.

   C. The missions both landed an orbiter on the surface.

   D. The missions were both unsuccessful.

15. What is a major idea found in both selections, "Early Exploration of Earth's Moon" and "Early Exploration of Mars"?

   A. no liquid found on the moon

   X B. less gravitational pull than Earth

   C. believed to be capable of supporting life

   D. closest Earth-like planet

Go On

16. Read this sentence.

"During these turbulent times, two tribe members gained *prominence* for their loyalty to the Seminoles."

The word *prominence* means the same as—

~~**A.**~~ being widely know.

B. being wealthy.

C. being free.

D. being able to self-govern.

17. Why did the Seminoles wait 23 years to organize their own government?

A. They wanted to be admitted as a state in the United States.

B. They did not want to have a formal government.

~~**C.**~~ They did not trust the United States.

D. They planned to move out of the United States.

18. Which of the following sentences from the article expresses an opinion?

A. "These battles began when bands of Creek Indians from Georgia and Alabama began to migrate south to Florida in order to escape conflicts with the Europeans."

B. "Although Abiaka was consistently pursued by the United States military, he continued to fight, to encourage Seminole warriors, and he refused to compromise or declare a truce."

C. "In 1934, Congress passed the Indian Reorganization Act, which allowed American Indians to conduct their own elections and govern their own affairs."

~~**D.**~~ "Survival in the swamp was difficult, even in the best circumstances."

5

During these turbulent times, two tribe members gained prominence for their loyalty to the Seminoles. Osceola's story is one of many legends. Osceola was a brave warrior whose genius outwitted the U. S. Army on many occasions. Osceola was lured to capture by General Thomas Jessup while under a flag of truce and later died in prison in South Carolina. The second famous leader of the Seminoles was a medicine man named Abiaka. He was a confident leader who was able to influence his fellow tribesmen to many battles against the United States, including the Battle of Okeechobee. His reign of influence began before Osceola's and he remained a prominent leader even after Osceola's capture and imprisonment. Although Abiaka was consistently pursued by the United States military, he continued to fight, to encourage Seminole warriors, and he refused to compromise or to declare a truce.

6

With the turn of a new century came many changes to the Seminole tribe. In 1934, Congress passed the Indian Reorganization Act, which allowed American Indians to conduct their own elections and govern their own affairs. The sorted history between the Seminoles and the U. S. government did much to deter the Seminoles from organizing their own government. However, in 1947 the Seminoles petitioned the United States for a settlement to cover their land losses during the three Seminole wars. Twenty-three years after the Indian Reorganization Act, the Seminoles officially organized their own government and became officially recognized as the Seminole Tribe of Florida. In 1970, the Indian Claims Commission of the United States awarded the Seminole Tribes of Oklahoma and Florida over $12 million as a settlement of the petition filed in 1947. This award was not collected until 1992.

7

Today, the Seminole Tribe of Florida continues to thrive. In recent years, the tribe has expanded its original business venture of "smoke shops" to include gaming enterprises, a hotel, entry into the citrus industry, and a collection of tourist attractions. These funds help to maintain the Seminole government and pay for such services as education, legal services, police services, and utilities. This has allowed the tribe to add two new reservations in Tampa and Immokalee. While the relationship between the United States and the Seminole Tribe of Florida has a long and difficult history, the citizens of the United States and the Seminole Tribe currently have a much more peaceful relationship, allowing the two governments and its citizens to work together. Today, after 12,000 years, the Seminole people continue to be true to their name by remaining a "free people."

Read this selection. Then answer the questions that follow.

Hound of the Baskervilles

by Sir Arthur Conan Doyle

Chapter 1
Mr. Sherlock Holmes

1   Mr. Sherlock Holmes, who was usually very late in the mornings, save upon those not infrequent occasions when he was up all night, was seated at the breakfast table. I stood upon the hearth-rug and picked up the stick which our visitor had left behind him the night before. It was a fine, thick piece of wood, bulbous-headed, of the sort which is known as a "Penang lawyer." Just under the head was a broad silver band nearly an inch across. "To James Mortimer, M.R.C.S., from his friends of the C.C.H.," was engraved upon it, with the date "1884." It was just such a stick as the old-fashioned family practitioner used to carry—dignified, solid, and reassuring.

2   "Well, Watson, what do you make of it?"

3   Holmes was sitting with his back to me, and I had given him no sign of my occupation.

4   "How did you know what I was doing? I believe you have eyes in the back of your head."

5   "I have, at least, a well-polished, silver-plated coffee-pot in front of me," said he. "But, tell me, Watson, what do you make of our visitor's stick? Since we have been so unfortunate as to miss him and have no notion of his errand, this accidental souvenir becomes of importance. Let me hear you reconstruct the man by an examination of it."

6   "I think," said I, following as far as I could the methods of my companion, "that Dr. Mortimer is a successful, elderly medical man, well-esteemed since those who know him give him this mark of their appreciation."

7   "Good!" said Holmes. "Excellent!"

8   "I think also that the probability is in favour of his being a country practitioner who does a great deal of his visiting on foot."

9   "Why so?"

10   "Because this stick, though originally a very handsome one has been so knocked about that I can hardly imagine a town practitioner carrying it. The thick-iron ferrule is worn down, so it is evident that he has done a great amount of walking with it."

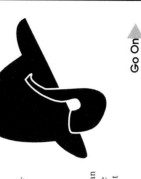

Go On ▲

---

19. Explain why the nickname "cimmaron" is appropriate for the Seminole Tribe of Florida.

Use details and information from the article to support your answer.

The nickname "cimmaron" is appropriate for the Seminole tribe because they are a free people with their own system of government. The Seminoles never surrendered or admitted defeat in their struggles against the United States government, even though the two groups battled for over 40 years.

20. What organizational pattern does the author use in this article?

A. The author compares the Seminole Tribe to the U.S. government.

B. The author presents the cause of the Seminoles' problems and then lists the effects.

X C. The author describes a series of events in the history of the Seminole tribe in chronological order.

D. The author describes the lifestyle of the Seminole Tribe of Florida.

Go On ▲

21. Read the sentence from the selection.

"...for I had often been *piqued* by his indifference to my admiration and to the attempts which I had made to give publicity to his methods."

What does the word *piqued* mean?

   A. feeling excitement or joy

 ✗ B. feeling resentment or annoyed

   C. feeling proud

   D. feeling sorrow or depression

22. How does Watson's conclusion about the visitor compare with Holmes' conclusion?

   A. Holmes agrees with Watson that the visitor was given the walking stick from a group of people who were given surgical assistance.

   B. Holmes agrees with Watson that the visitor is a successful, elderly man who is well esteemed in his medical practice.

 ✗ C. Holmes agrees with Watson that the visitor is a country practitioner and he walks a great deal.

   D. Holmes does not agree with any of Watson's conclusions.

Go On

---

11   "Perfectly sound!" said Holmes.

12   "And then again, there is the 'friends of the C.C.H.' I should guess that to be the Something Hunt, the local hunt to whose members he has possibly given some surgical assistance, and which has made him a small presentation in return."

13   "Really, Watson, you excel yourself," said Holmes, pushing back his chair and lighting a cigarette. "I am bound to say that in all the accounts which you have been so good as to give of my own small achievements you have habitually underrated your own abilities. It may be that you are not yourself luminous, but you are a conductor of light. Some people without possessing genius have a remarkable power of stimulating it. I confess, my dear fellow, that I am very much in your debt."

14   He had never said as much before, and I must admit that his words gave me keen pleasure, for I had often been piqued by his indifference to my admiration and to the attempts which I had made to give publicity to his methods. I was proud, too, to think that I had so far mastered his system as to apply it in a way which earned his approval. He now took the stick from my hands and examined it for a few minutes with his naked eyes. Then with an expression of interest he laid down his cigarette, and carrying the cane to the window, he looked over it again with a convex lens.

15   "Interesting, though elementary," said he as he returned to his favourite corner of the settee¹. "There are certainly one or two indications upon the stick. It gives us the basis for several deductions."

16   "Has anything escaped me?" I asked with some self-importance. "I trust that there is nothing of consequence which I have overlooked?"

17   "I am afraid, my dear Watson, that most of your conclusions were erroneous². When I said that you stimulated me I meant, to be frank, that in noting your fallacies I was occasionally guided towards the truth. Not that you are entirely wrong in this instance. The man is certainly a country practitioner. And he walks a good deal."

18   "Then I was right."

19   "To that extent."

20   "But that was all."

21   "No, no, my dear Watson, not all—by no means all."

¹ settee: a comfortable seat for two or more people, with a cushioned back and arms
² erroneous: incorrect or based on an incorrect assumption

Go On

---

26. Which statement is the most important conclusion the reader can draw from the selection, "Hound of the Baskervilles"?

    A. Holmes and Watson do not get along and will no longer work together.

    X **B.** Holmes and Watson will work together to figure out information about the owner of the walking stick.

    C. Holmes and Watson cannot work together because Holmes does not think Watson is smart.

    D. Holmes and Watson will work together, but will not share ideas.

27. How might this story have been different if it was told from a third-person point of view?

    A. Watson would be narrating the story.

    B. Holmes would be narrating the story.

    X **C.** The story would use proper names and pronouns such as "he" in the narrative.

    D. The story would use proper names and pronouns and include each character's personal thoughts.

Go On ▲

---

23. How does Holmes feel about Watson?

    A. Holmes dislikes Watson.

    X **B.** Holmes thinks he is smarter than Watson.

    C. Holmes thinks Watson is smarter than him.

    D. Holmes does not think Watson is a good detective.

24. Why does Watson evaluate the walking stick?

    A. He wants to figure out why it was left behind.

    B. He wants to make one for himself.

    C. He wants to have Holmes tell him if he's wrong about its owner.

    X **D.** He wants to impress Holmes with his investigative skills.

25. Why did the author use Watson's point-of-view to tell the story?

    A. The author uses this point-of-view because Watson is a better detective than Holmes.

    X **B.** The author creates suspense with this point-of-view because the reader can't tell what Holmes is thinking.

    C. The author uses this point-of-view because it is not important what Holmes thinks in this story.

    D. This point-of-view is best because Watson does most of the talking in this story.

Go On ▲

Read this selection. Then answer the questions that follow.

The Prince and the Pauper
by Mark Twain

Chapter I.
The Birth of the Prince and the Pauper.

1   In the ancient city of London, on a certain autumn day in the second quarter of the sixteenth century, a boy was born to a poor family of the name of Canty, who did not want him. On the same day another English child was born to a rich family of the name of Tudor, who did want him. All England wanted him too. England had so longed for him, and hoped for him, and prayed God for him, that, now that he was really come, the people went nearly mad for joy. Mere acquaintances hugged and kissed each other and cried. Everybody took a holiday, and high and low, rich and poor, feasted and danced and sang, and got very mellow; and they kept this up for days and nights together. By day, London was a sight to see, with gay banners waving from every balcony and housetop, and splendid pageants marching along. By night, it was again a sight to see, with its great bonfires at every corner, and its troops of revellers making merry around them. There was no talk in all England but of the new baby, Edward Tudor, Prince of Wales, who lay lapped in silks and satins, unconscious of all this fuss, and not knowing that great lords and ladies were tending him and watching over him—and not caring, either. But there was no talk about the other baby, Tom Canty, lapped in his poor rags, except among the family of paupers whom he had just come to trouble with his presence.

*****

2   By-and-by Tom's reading and dreaming about princely life wrought such a strong effect upon him that he began to ACT the prince, unconsciously. His speech and manners became curiously ceremonious and courtly, to the vast admiration and amusement of his intimates. But Tom's influence among these young people began to grow now, day by day; and in time he came to be looked up to, by them, with a sort of wondering awe, as a superior being. He seemed to know so much! and he could do and say such marvelous things! and withal, he was so deep and wise! Tom's remarks, and Tom's performances, were reported by the boys to their elders; and these, also, presently began to discuss Tom Canty, and to regard him as a most gifted and extraordinary creature. Full-grown people brought their perplexities to Tom for solution, and were often astonished at the wit and wisdom of his decisions. In fact he was become a hero to all who knew him except his own family—these, only, saw nothing in him.

Go On

---

3   Privately, after a while, Tom organized a royal court! He was the prince; his special comrades were guards, chamberlains, equerries, lords and ladies in waiting, and the royal family. Daily the mock prince was received with elaborate ceremonials borrowed by Tom from his romantic readings; daily the great affairs of the mimic kingdom were discussed in the royal council, and daily his mimic highness issued decrees to his imaginary armies, navies, and viceroyalties.

4   After which, he would go forth in his rags and beg a few farthings, eat his poor crust, take his customary cuffs and abuse, and then stretch himself upon his handful of foul straw, and resume his empty grandeurs in his dreams.

5   And still his desire to look just once upon a real prince, in the flesh, grew upon him, day by day, and week by week, until at last it absorbed all other desires, and became the one passion of his life.

6   One January day, on his usual begging tour, he tramped despondently up and down the region round about Mincing Lane and Little East Cheap, hour after hour, barefooted and cold, looking in at cook-shop windows and longing for the dreadful pork-pies and other deadly inventions displayed there—for to him these were dainties fit for the angels; that is, judging by the smell, they were—for it had never been his good luck to own and eat one. There was a cold drizzle of rain; the atmosphere was murky; it was a melancholy day. At night Tom reached home so wet and tired and hungry that it was not possible for his father and grandmother to observe his forlorn condition and not be moved—after their fashion; wherefore they gave him a brisk cuffing[1] at once and sent him to bed. For a long time his pain and hunger, and the swearing and fighting going on in the building, kept him awake; but at last his thoughts drifted away to far, romantic lands, and he fell asleep in the company of jewelled and gilded princelings who live in vast palaces, and had servants salaaming[2] before them or flying to execute their orders. And then, as usual, he dreamed that HE was a princeling himself. All night long the glories of his royal estate shone upon him; he moved among great lords and ladies, in a blaze of light, breathing perfumes, drinking in delicious music, and answering the reverent obeisances[3] of the glittering throng as it parted to make way for him, with here a smile, and there a nod of his princely head. And when he awoke in the morning and looked upon the wretchedness about him, his dream had had its usual effect—it had intensified the sordidness of his surroundings a thousandfold. Then came bitterness, and heartbreak, and tears.

[1] cuffing: to strike with an open hand
[2] salaaming: a respectful greeting
[3] obeisances: a gesture of respect or reverence, such as a bow or curtsy

Go On

---

28. You are writing an essay on how Mark Twain uses imagery in "The Prince and the Pauper." Which is the **best** example of Mark Twain's use of imagery?

A. "Full-grown people brought their perplexities to Tom for solution, and were often astonished at the wit and wisdom of his decisions."

B. "And then, as usual, he dreamed that HE was a princeling himself."

C. "His speech and manners became curiously ceremonious and courtly, to the vast admiration and amusement of his intimates."

X D. "After which, he would go forth in his rags and beg a few farthlings, eat his poor crust, take his customary cuffs and abuse, and then stretch himself upon his handful of foul straw, and resume his empty grandeurs in his dreams."

29. In paragraph 6 of the story, why does the author include how Tom's father and grandmother treated him when he got home?

A. to show how much Tom enjoyed his home life

B. to show how much Tom was loved by his family

C. to show why Tom wanted to sleep at home

X D. to show why Tom dreamt about a different life

Go On

30. Does the author compare or contrast Tom and Edward in the first paragraph?

A. He compares the two boys to show they are similar.

B. He compares the two boys to show they are different.

C. He contrasts the two boys to show they are similar.

X D. He contrasts the two boys to show they are different.

31. Which sentence tells how Tom Canty and Edward Tudor are alike?

A. They are both rich.

B. They live in the same house.

C. They both have parents who want them.

X D. They have the same birthday.

32. What literary device does the author use in the first paragraph of the story?

X A. foreshadowing

B. flashback

C. simile

D. metaphor

33. What purpose does the author's description of Tom's family serve to the mood of the story?

A. It explains why Tom enjoyed his home life.

B. It explains how much Tom was loved by his family.

C. It explains why Tom wanted to sleep at home.

X D. It explains why Tom dreamt about having a different life.

Go On

Florence Nightingale

1   Born on May 12, 1820, Florence Nightingale was named for the city of her birth: Florence, Italy. The second daughter born to wealthy parents, Florence enjoyed a life of privilege. During her childhood, the Nightingales divided their time between two homes in England: Lea Hurst in Derbyshire during the summer months and Embley in Hampshire for the winter.

2   Florence's father was educated at Cambridge University. He taught both his daughters at home. Florence enjoyed studying and learning, while her sister Parthenope preferred artistic endeavors, such as painting and needlework. The Nightingales were admired members of high society, and it was believed Florence would make an excellent wife and socialite. Florence, however, had other plans.

3   Interested in social plight rather than social graces, Florence visited the sick and the poor. She made trips to hospitals and to homes of the sick. She investigated nursing techniques and medicine. Florence's interests were quite disheartening to her parents. Nursing was not considered a suitable profession for well-educated women in the mid-nineteenth century. Yet, Florence persevered.

4   In the early 1850s, Florence underwent three months of nurse training at Kaiserworth, a German school and hospital. By 1853, Florence had been become the Superintendent of the London Establishment for Gentlewomen During Illness.

5   In March 1854, Britain, France, and Turkey declared war on Russia. The Russian troops were defeated at the Battle of Alma by September, but news reports harshly criticized British medical facilities. Florence was deeply moved and organized a party of 38 nurses to care for troops. The nurses arrived in Turkey by November, where medical services were insufficient and ineffective. At first, the male doctors resented the women nurses, but Florence's diplomacy and an onslaught of wounded united the group. Florence's caring touch and tact earned her much respect. Troops practices were studied and implemented. Florence was an advocate of cleaner conditions, improved facilities, and better patient care.

6   Her arguments cemented her reputation as the founder of modern nursing. The much-loved nurse returned home in 1856, soon after the war ended. In November of that year, she became an advocate for the improvement of soldiers' health. She was appointed chairperson of the Royal Commission and investigated the health of the British Army. Florence's participation led to improvements in barracks and hospitals. She was considered an expert on military and civilian sanitation.

7   Florence Nightingale wrote several books and manuals on nursing practice and helped to establish training schools for young nurses. Although the physical toll of the war ravaged[1] Florence, she worked tirelessly to improve health standards. Florence was an important female role model during the male-dominated 1800s. In 1883, Florence was awarded the Royal Red Cross by Queen Victoria, and in 1907, she became the first woman to be honored with the Order of Merit.

8   Florence Nightingale died at the age of 90 on August 13, 1910. Although she never had any children of her own, she lovingly referred to the British Army as "my children." Today, Florence is still considered one of the most influential women in history.

[1] ravaged: a destructive effect

Go On

37. Which statement **best** summarizes the passage, "Florence Nightingale"?

✗A. Florence Nightingale greatly impacted the field of nursing.

B. Florence Nightingale was awarded the Royal Red Cross.

C. Florence Nightingale's family did not want her to become a nurse.

D. Florence Nightingale wrote several books on nursing practices.

38. Which event happened first in Florence's life?

A. She returned home after the war ended.

✗B. She became Superintendent of the London Establishment for Gentlewomen During Illness.

C. She organized a group of 38 nurses to care for troops.

D. She was awarded and honored with the Order of Merit.

Go On

---

34. The author probably wrote this passage to—

A. entertain readers with a story about nursing.

B. explain how to become a nurse.

✗C. describe Florence's achievements in nursing.

D. persuade readers to investigate nursing.

35. Read the sentence from the selection.

"Interested in social *plight*, rather than social graces, Florence visited the sick and the poor."

What does the word *plight* mean?

A. extremes

B. gatherings

✗C. conditions

D. status

36. The reader can conclude that—

A. Florence's parents were initially pleased with her choice in nursing.

B. women could not work outside the home.

C. women did not affect history.

✗D. women's roles were limited in the 19th century.

Go On

Assessment Two

Show What You Know® on the Common Core for Grade 8 Reading

39. According to the passage, what event prompted Florence Nightingale to organize a party of 38 nurses?

A. her appointment as Superintendent of the London Establishment for Gentlewomen During Illness

X B. the criticism of British medical facilities after the Battle of Alma

C. her completion of nurse training at Kaiserworth

D. the Royal Red Cross she was awarded by Queen Victoria

40. The fifth paragraph is mostly about—

X A. Florence's part in providing quality care to troops.

B. the defeat of the Russian troops by Turkey.

C. the disapproval of women nurses by male doctors.

D. the troops naming Florence "Lady with the Lamp."

1 Ⓐ Ⓑ ● Ⓓ

2 Ⓐ Ⓑ ● Ⓓ

3

From the title of the story, the reader knows the judge is a wise woman. Since the judge is wise, it is unlikely she would waste her time with a silly request, such as asking the shack to speak. The reader should realize the judge had a greater purpose. It turns out, in this story, she did. She knew asking the shack to talk would make observers laugh. Since laughing in the courtroom was against the rules, the judge fined the people in garlic, so Chang Fu-Yen could find his crop.

4 Ⓐ ● Ⓒ Ⓓ

5 ● Ⓑ Ⓒ Ⓓ

6 ● Ⓑ Ⓒ Ⓓ

7 Ⓐ Ⓑ ● Ⓓ

8

> Both Chang Fu-Yen and the farmer trust each judge they go to for help. In "The Wise Judge," Chang Fu-Yen brings the shack to court and takes it apart when the judge asks him to, even though he does not understand why. In "A Wise Judge's Sentence," the farmer agrees to follow the judge's advice by giving the hunter's sons each a lamb instead of having the judge punish the hunter.

9  Ⓐ Ⓑ Ⓒ ●

10

> People should continue to make donations to fund the space program because man has always been interested in the moon and stars. Man's exploration of the moon has allowed us to find ways to put humans in space. It has allowed us to create and build new machines on Earth for space travel and space exploration, such as the space shuttle. Space exploration has also allowed us to collect moon rock samples, giving us information on the formation and history of the universe.

11 Ⓐ Ⓑ Ⓒ ●

12 ● Ⓑ Ⓒ Ⓓ

13 ● Ⓑ Ⓒ Ⓓ

14 Ⓐ ● Ⓒ Ⓓ

15 Ⓐ ● Ⓒ Ⓓ

16 ● Ⓑ Ⓒ Ⓓ

17 Ⓐ Ⓑ ● Ⓓ

18 Ⓐ Ⓑ Ⓒ ●

19

The nickname "cimmaron" is appropriate for the Seminole tribe because they are a free people with their own system of government. The Seminoles never surrendered or admitted defeat in their struggles against the United States government, even though the two groups battled for over 40 years.

20 (A) (B) ● (D)

21 (A) ● (C) (D)

22 (A) (B) ● (D)

23 (A) ● (C) (D)

24 (A) (B) (C) ●

25 (A) ● (C) (D)

26 (A) ● (C) (D)

27 (A) (B) ● (D)

28 (A) (B) (C) ●

29 (A) (B) (C) ●

30 (A) (B) (C) ●

31 (A) (B) (C) ●

32 ● (B) (C) (D)

33 (A) (B) (C) ●

34 (A) (B) ● (D)

35 (A) (B) ● (D)

36 (A) (B) (C) ●

37 ● (B) (C) (D)

38 (A) ● (C) (D)

39 (A) ● (C) (D)

40 ● (B) (C) (D)

Question	Standard	Answer	Keywords
1	RL.8.3	C	Cause and Effect
2	RL.8.2	C	Theme
3	RL.8.1	—	Support
4	RL.8.4	B	Foreshadowing
5	RL.8.10	A	Author's Purpose
6	RL.8.4	A	Figurative Language
7	RL.8.2	C	Central Idea
8	RL.8.5	—	Compare and Contrast across Texts
9	RI.8.6	D	Author's Purpose
10	RI.8.10	—	Extend Information
11	RI.8.2	D	Main Idea
12	RI.8.3	A	Make Connections
13	RI.8.1	A	Cite Textual Evidence
14	RI.8.1	B	Cite Textual Evidence
15	RI.8.3	B	Main Ideas
16	RI.8.4	A	Analyze Words
17	RI.8.3	C	Cause and Effect
18	RI.8.8	D	Fact and Opinion
19	RI.8.1	—	Interpret Information
20	RI.8.5	C	Organization

—see analysis for constructed response

Question	Standard	Answer	Keywords
21	RL.8.4	B	Analyze Words
22	RL.8.1	C	Cite Textual Evidence
23	RL.8.1	B	Inferences
24	RL.8.3	D	Making Connections
25	RL.8.6	B	Point of View
26	RL.8.1	B	Draw Conclusions
27	RL.8.6	C	Point of View
28	RL.8.4	D	Analyze Words
29	RL.8.3	D	Author's Purpose
30	RL.8.10	D	Compare and Contrast
31	RL.8.1	D	Compare
32	RL.8.4	A	Literary Device
33	RL.8.3	D	Mood
34	RI.8.6	C	Author's Purpose
35	RI.8.4	C	Define Words
36	RI.8.1	D	Draw Conclusions
37	RI.8.2	A	Central Idea/Summary
38	RI.8.3	B	Sequences
39	RI.8.3	B	Cause and Effect
40	RI.8.5	A	Analyze Paragraph

—see analysis for constructed response

Reading Assessment Two: Correlation Chart

Use this chart to identify areas for improvement for individual students or for the class as a whole. For example, enter students' names in the left-hand column. When a student misses a question, place an "X" in the corresponding box. A column with a large number of "Xs" shows that the class needs more practice with that particular objective.

Correlation	RL.8.3	RL.8.2	RL.8.1	RL.8.4	RL.8.10	RL.8.4	RL.8.2	RL.8.5	RI.8.6	RI.8.10	RI.8.2	RI.8.3	RI.8.1	RI.8.1	RI.8.3	RI.8.4	RI.8.3	RI.8.8	RI.8.1	RI.8.5
Answer	C	C	—	B	A	A	C	—	D	—	D	A	A	B	B	A	C	D	—	C
Question	1	2	3	4	5	6	7	8	9	10	11	12	13	14	15	16	17	18	19	20

Student Names

—*see analysis for constructed response*

Reading Assessment Two: Correlation Chart

Correlation	RL.8.4	RL.8.1	RL.8.1	RL.8.3	RL.8.6	RL.8.1	RL.8.6	RL.8.4	RL.8.3	RL.8.10	RL.8.1	RL.8.4	RL.8.3	RI.8.6	RI.8.1	RI.8.1	RI.8.2	RI.8.3	RI.8.3	RI.8.5
Answer	B	C	B	D	B	B	C	D	D	D	D	A	D	C	C	D	A	B	B	A
Question	21	22	23	24	25	26	27	28	29	30	31	32	33	34	35	36	37	38	39	40

Student Names

—see analysis for constructed response

For most state proficiency tests, students will answer multiple-choice, short-answer, and extended-response questions.

Multiple-Choice Items: Multiple-choice items have four answer choices, and only one is correct. Multiple-choice items are usually worth one point each. An item with no response will be automatically counted as incorrect.

Short-Answer Items: Short-answer items will require students to write a word, a phrase, or a sentence or two. Student responses receive a score of 0, 1, or 2 points. Each short-answer item has an item-specific scoring guideline. Here is a 2-point short-answer scoring rubric sample:

A **2-point response** provides a complete interpretation and/or correct solution. It demonstrates a thorough understanding of the concept or task. It indicates logical reasoning and conclusions. It is accurate, relevant, and complete.

A **1-point response** provides evidence of a partial interpretation and/or solution process. It demonstrates an incomplete understanding of the concept or task. It contains minor flaws in reasoning. It neglects to address some aspect of the task.

A **Zero-point response** does not meet the criteria required to earn one point. The response indicates inadequate understanding of the task and/or the idea or concept needed to answer the item. It may only repeat information given in the test item. The response may provide an incorrect solution/response and the provided supportive information may be totally irrelevant to the item, or possibly, no other information is shown. The student may have written on a different topic or written, "I don't know."

Extended-Response Items: Extended-response items usually require students to write a complete sentence or a short paragraph. Student responses receive a score of 0, 1, 2, 3, or 4 points. Each item has an item-specific scoring guideline. Here is a 4-point extended-response scoring rubric sample:

A **4-point response** provides essential aspects of a complete interpretation and/or a correct solution. The response thoroughly addresses the points relevant to the concept or task. It provides strong evidence that information, reasoning, and conclusions have a definite logical relationship. It is clearly focused and organized, showing relevance to the concept, task and/or solution process.

A **3-point response** provides essential elements of an interpretation and/or a solution. It addresses the points relevant to the concept or task. It provides ample evidence that information, reasoning, and conclusions have a logical relationship. It is focused and organized, showing relevance to the concept, task, or solution process.

A **2-point response** provides a partial interpretation and/or solution. It somewhat addresses the points relevant to the concept or task. It provides some evidence that information, reasoning, and conclusions have a relationship. It is relevant to the concept and/or task, but there are gaps in focus and organization.

A **1-point response** provides an unclear, inaccurate interpretation and/or solution. It fails to address or omits significant aspects of the concept or task. It provides unrelated or unclear evidence that information, reasoning, and conclusions have a relationship. There is little evidence of focus or organization relevant to the concept, task, and /or solution process.

A **Zero-point response** does not meet the criteria required to earn one point. The response indicates inadequate understanding of the task and/or the idea or concept needed to answer the item. It may only repeat information given in the test item. The response may provide an incorrect solution/response and the provided supportive information may be totally irrelevant to the item, or possibly, no other information is shown. The student may have written on a different topic or written, "I don't know."

Notes

Notes

Show What You Know® on the COMMON CORE

Assessing Student Knowledge of the Common Core State Standards (CCSS)
Reading • Mathematics • Grades 3–8

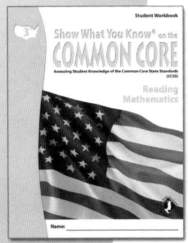

Diagnostic Test-Preparation Student Workbooks and Parent/Teacher Editions for Grades 3–5

Single Subject Student Workbooks and Parent/Teacher Editions for Grades 6–8

For more information, call our toll-free number: 1.877.PASSING (727.7464)
or visit our website: www.showwhatyouknowpublishing.com